Teaching
Reading Strategies
in the Primary Grades

Engaging Lessons and Activities That Help Young Students
Learn Key Reading Strategies—and Become Independent Readers

**By Bette S. Bergeron and
Melody Bradbury-Wolff**

SCHOLASTIC
PROFESSIONAL BOOKS

New York • Toronto • London • Auckland • Sydney
Mexico City • New Delhi • Hong Kong • Buenos Aires

*This book is lovingly
dedicated to our husbands,
Don and Greg*

Acknowledgements

We are grateful for the support, advice, and encouragement of many people who made this book possible. First, we would like to thank the children and parents with whom we've had the privilege of working and from whom we have learned so much about teaching, ourselves, and insights about childhood.

We would also like to thank:

❂ Mark Kellogg, administrator extraordinaire, for challenging us and supporting our endeavors.

❂ The wonderful support staff that helped us implement and refine our strategy instruction.

❂ Barb Krivickas, for her literacy expertise.

❂ Deedee, Renee, Sher, Jane, Chrissy, Debbie, Becky, and Brenda for their insight and friendship.

❂ Carrie Monzin, who we are confident will become an exceptional educator.

❂ Our editors, Jeanette Moss and Wendy Murray, who believed in our vision and encouraged its development.

Finally, we would like to thank our families for their unconditional support and belief that anything is possible with love, guidance, and patience—especially our parents, Harlan and Kay Sylvester and Charlotte Bradbury, who were and continue to be our finest teachers. This book is also written in memory of Jerry Bradbury, who was there when our book began and who continues to guide us in our journey.

Front cover design by Josué Castilleja

Cover Photograph by S.O.D.A.

Interior Design by Sydney Wright

Edited by Jeanette Moss

ISBN: 0-439-28840-1

Contents

Preface

This book grew out of a friendship between a classroom teacher (Melody) and a college professor (Bette). Besides many common interests, ranging from aerobics to an obsession with cats, we found that we shared a passion for teaching reading. We also shared a deep concern for our profession and those responsible for guiding the development of the youngest learners. Both of us knew intuitively that teachers need a variety of tools to meet the academic and developmental needs of emerging readers, and we also recognized that the

▲ Strategies-based literacy learning creates independent readers.

challenge lies in making these tools accessible to teachers so they can make effective instructional decisions for their young learners.

We met in a graduate literacy class Bette was teaching. One goal of the class was to encourage the graduate students to develop a classroom action-research project that would help them wrestle with an issue related to literacy. Before taking the class, Melody had been searching out professional resources to help her become more effective as a primary grade teacher. This independent inquiry led to one component of effective instruction that Melody would use as the focus for her graduate action-research project—the application of strategies. By determining which strategies her most proficient students used and being guided by that knowledge, she would develop a plan for all the children in her classroom.

✳

This initial inquiry led to a three-year collaboration during which we refined those strategies and determined how to integrate them into Melody's daily literacy instruction. Although Melody's students are first graders, this instructional focus is applicable to a wide range of learning levels, and the suggestions in this book are intended for teachers across the primary grades. We've set up the book to include a variety of useful resources in each chapter. For example, we provide *What the Experts Say About . . .* sections that overview current research on a variety of topics covered in the book. We hope that these short pieces will not only help guide teachers, but that they can use them to share information on best practices with school administrators, school boards, and parents. We have seen the value of sharing this important information with other education stakeholders in order to provide support for the instructional decisions we make.

Although the focus of the book is on instruction in Grades K to 3, each chapter includes *Expansions* and *Variations* that will provide a variety of ideas for extending activities for both accelerated and struggling learners. Besides helping teachers adapt the strategy activities across a range of grade levels, the approach acknowledges the reality that all teachers must meet a wide range of learning needs and levels within a single classroom. Each chapter also includes *Checking Up on Learning* and reproducible instructional materials to provide teachers with ideas on how to assess students' learning and to implement the activities outlined in the chapters.

In recognition of the critical role that parents and guardians play in the academic development of young children, each chapter includes *Send-Home Ideas* to involve caregivers in literacy learning. The *Letters Home* conclude each chapter and not only explain strategy learning for parents but also provide an overview of the chapter's contents.

We are excited about sharing our experiences in strategies-based literacy learning! We hope that this book provides teachers with ideas to enhance their instruction and enrich the life of each child they teach.

Reading Strategies
What? Why? How?

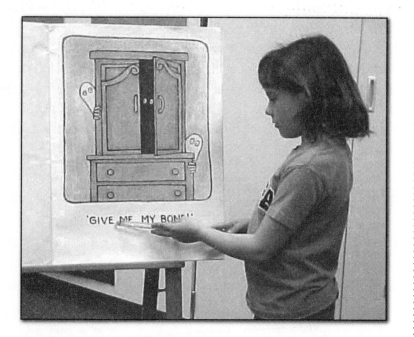

'GIVE ME MY BONE!'

Strategic Reading—An Overview

Our struggle to answer questions about the best instructional practices for young learners has led us to teach techniques that focus on strategies instead of isolated skills. Strategies are the processes for using skills effectively within the context of reading. For example, a reader might understand the skill involved with putting the letters *b* and *l* together to make /bl/ when prompted to do so by a teacher. A strategic reader recognizes when to use this strategy of *blending*, along with a repertoire of other strategies, when independently reading a book for the first time.

We've found that by emphasizing strategies, we can bring emerging readers to the point of independence. This approach requires using a variety of developmentally appropriate techniques, focusing on meeting each child's individual needs, and giving young learners the tools—or strategies—they need to become successful, independent readers.

In this first chapter, we'll define the instruction and classroom environment that supports the teaching and use of reading strategies. In subsequent chapters, we'll explore a variety of classroom activities that reinforce the use of strategies in different literacy contexts—including word study and shared reading.

It's difficult to explain how readers use strategies because good readers draw on them internally and automatically. Strategic readers think to themselves about reading in ways that enhance and build understanding. This thinking about thinking (metacognition) is ordinarily an invisible process, and consequently it is difficult to observe. Therefore, to help children develop and use strategies automatically teachers have to bring them to the surface—externalize them by saying aloud what they are thinking before, during, and

What the Experts Say About . . .

Teaching Reading Strategies

Students who receive effective strategy instruction score significantly higher on standardized tests of reading comprehension, reasoning, and self-esteem.

The metacognitive processes of thinking about thinking, thinking about reading, and constructing meaning are central to strategy instruction. To use reading strategies, students must apply a variety of concepts across many reading contexts. Successful instruction includes the following:

Teacher modeling. Combine explicit, direct instruction with student-generated examples, discussion, and elaboration while demonstrating the strategies by reading or thinking aloud.

Scaffolding. Build from what students know; start instruction where your students are right now. Familiar information is used as the scaffold to build up to new strategy use.

Group practice. After explicit instruction, pairs or small groups read texts at their level and practice using the strategies that have been taught. The goal is to increase students' independent use of strategies.

Peer teaching. Invite students to become the teacher and talk to their classmates through the thinking process.

Integration. Infuse formal reading instruction and informal contexts (writing, read-alouds, and so on) with strategy talk, as students begin to recognize strategies as a tool for their own learning.

Sources: Baumann and Ivey, 1997; Block and Graham, 1993; Fitzpatrick, 1998; Paris, Lipson, and Wixson, 1994; Ross, 1999.

after reading. This explicit modeling is critical to teaching strategies effectively. However, it's important to remember that the focus in teaching strategies is, ultimately, on generating meaning —whether concentrating on words or word parts or analyzing entire passages. Children need to have a purpose for reading—they must have a desire to learn and to understand what they read. It is one of a teacher's many responsibilities to help foster this desire and keep it in focus when choosing and teaching strategies.

Selecting Strategies to Teach

You can teach each of the specific strategies described in the chart below as part of many different reading tasks. Appendix 1 on page 160 also contains a chart of the various strategies along with the instructional techniques and activities you can use to teach them. Reading strategies generally fall under the following categories:

- **Timing.** Some strategies, such as accessing, work best before reading a passage. Others, such as *synthesizing* or *summarizing*, are effective after a text is read.

- **Level.** Some strategies are more appropriate than others for certain developmental levels. Emerging readers, for example, may first focus on word-level strategies such as *forming* and *tracking*. But as readers become more proficient, they should advance to higher-level thinking, focusing on **text-level** strategies such as analyzing and monitoring.

- **Text depth.** Strategies also vary according to the depth of text addressed. For example, some strategies are more appropriate when attending to word features. *Chunking* and *sliding*, for example, help the reader decode difficult words. *Focusing* and *visualizing* are more appropriate for text-level comprehension.

The following chart gives a brief summary of the strategies covered and notes whether they are appropriate for word-level or text-level instruction or both.

Building fluency (Text level)	**Reading like you talk—focusing on fluency when reading aloud:** Building fluency also occurs when children reread a familiar story. Building fluency bolsters confidence in reading while also focusing readers on the phrasing in a text.
Checking (Word level)	**Checking picture cues to assist in decoding a difficult word:** When encountering an unknown word, readers can use available illustrations as one clue for determining what would make sense for that particular word.
Chunking (Word level)	**Analyzing words by breaking them into decodable parts; recognizing chunks or patterns sound:** Chunking emphasizes the use of patterns found in word *onsets* (the initial letter sounds in a word up to the first vowel) and *rimes* (the part or chunk of the word that follows).
Confirming (Word/Text)	**Using cues to determine if a word sounds right; accepting the appropriateness of the response:** After attempting to correct a miscue, the reader confirms that this attempt "sounds right" (and makes sense) in the context of the sentence or the story.
Cross-Checking (Word/Text)	**Using resources in the learning environment, such as environmental print, as a reference to confirm a guess:** Students often cross-check using the Word Wall, which contains familiar sight words, when reading a new text.
Focusing (Text level)	**Distinguishing between important and unimportant information in a text:** Students can be prompted to focus on new facts on a topic in a nonfiction text, or on the sequence of events in a fictional story. Focusing guides the reader to concentrate on what is most important in bringing meaning to that text.
Forming sounds (Word level)	**Getting your mouth ready to read; focusing on how the mouth is shaped to produce sounds for certain letter cues or patterns:** This strategy is particularly effective with very young readers, who are just learning sound-symbol relationships.
Monitoring (Text level)	**Monitoring for understanding by checking to see if the text makes sense:** Monitoring is often modeled after a miscue is made by stopping to ask the reader, "Did that make sense?"
Predicting (Text level)	**Using the title and cover illustration to predict what will happen in the text; anticipating content based on prior knowledge:** Predicting usually occurs when a new story is introduced. It helps the reader focus on important elements in the text in order to facilitate understanding of that text.
Previewing (Text level)	**Getting an overview of text structure, text cues, pictures, and personal experiences prior to reading a text:** Previewing could include taking a "picture walk" prior to reading that text, briefly discussing the illustrations. Previewing also takes advantage of special features in a text, such as font changes or special phrasing.
Questioning (Word/Text)	**Asking questions of yourself as you read to monitor for understanding:** Questioning can focus on individual words ("What familiar chunks do I see in this word?") or on the overall meaning of the text ("Did that makes sense?").
Rereading (Word/Text)	**Rereading a portion of a text to build fluency; rereading to use context to correct a miscue or make meaning:** By rereading a phrase or sentence after making a miscue, readers can check to see if their correction makes sense in the context of that particular

sentence or story. When rereading an entire story, children will build, confidence with that text and will become more fluent in their reading.

Self-Correcting (Word/Text)	**Repairing faulty comprehension by correcting a miscue or part of a text:** Self-correcting occurs when readers independently discover an error that they have made while reading and attempt to correct that miscue on their own.
Skipping (Word level)	**Omitting a difficult word that's not needed to maintain meaning—and continuing to read:** Skipping words allows the reader to continue reading the text without interrupting fluency or losing overall meaning.
Sliding (Word level)	**Beginning with the onset of a word and sliding to the end to help with decoding:** Sliding focuses the reader on initial word sounds as one cue for figuring out difficult words, and then using the end sound as a confirming clue.
Stretching (Word level)	**Stretching out each sound of a word in sequence in order to read it:** Stretching focuses the reader on distinct sounds or patterns within a difficult word as the reader slowly "sounds out" the word.
Summarizing (Text level)	**Identifying the text sequence or important parts of a text after reading:** Summarizing after a story or chapter is completed focuses the reader on the overall meaning of the text.
Synthesizing (Text level)	**Integrating information within and across a text; bringing together separate elements of a text to make a connected and meaningful whole:** For example, groups of children could search a text for different story elements, and then together the class would synthesize all of the information gathered.
Thinking Aloud (Text level)	**Orally commenting on your thinking processes as you read to maintain or model comprehension:** When reading aloud to a class, the teacher can think aloud by stopping at various points in the text to discuss what strategies are being used to maintain comprehension of the story. Thinking aloud provides a way to verbalize metacognition, which is the process of thinking about what a reader is thinking.
Tracking (or Pointing) (Word level)	**Using voice-to-print correspondence to match a word read aloud with a word in print, usually by pointing or voice emphasis:** Tracking is often modeled using an enlarged version of a story. As the story is read, the text is tracked with a pointer. Tracking helps readers make connections between words being read and what is printed in a text.
Visualizing (Word level)	**Creating mental visual images to keep your mind focused as you read or listen:** Visualizing helps readers with comprehension by conjuring up images of a story as it is being read.
Accessing (Text level)	**Accessing background knowledge to search for connections between what is known and new information in the text:** When introducing a new text, the teacher may ask students to access what they already know about the topic to be explored in the book. Students also access their own experiences to compare with events or characters portrayed.
Analyzing (Text level)	**Analyzing a text for story elements, including characters, events, setting:** Story elements can be analyzed in various ways, by drawing diagrams to compare stories, mapping out events, or illustrating settings. Analyzing provides more in-depth knowledge about the text.

The following hints will help guide your strategy selection:

1. **Select just a few strategies at a time to guide instruction.** Selections will depend on a variety of factors, including the developmental level of individual students, the type of text to be read, and even your own district's standards. Your selections can shift over time as students gain independence in strategy use.

   ○ For example, at the beginning of first grade, we focus on refining the *checking* and *tracking* strategies that the children have been introduced to in kindergarten. The more fluent readers are already using *chunking* and *stretching* strategies when they encounter difficult words.

2. **Continually analyze students' mistakes to determine what strategies they use when they encounter difficult text.** As you analyze, you can modify your repertoire of strategies to match students' needs. Observing children is critical to careful planning for strategy instruction.

3. **Target those strategies that are the best fit for a particular group of young learners and their previous strategy instruction.** By starting with familiar strategies and building to those that the children can use immediately, you can provide scaffolding for success.

   ○ When establishing a plan for first grade children, for instance, we initially set aside strategies such as *confirming* and *monitoring* because these were too difficult for young children to observe directly. However, we decided that others, such as *forming*, seemed more developmentally appropriate for a kindergarten class. Therefore, we decided to begin our strategies lessons by reviewing the *forming* strategy, which was already familiar to our readers, and then built quickly to word-level strategies such as *chunking* and *stretching* to build confidence.

4. **In order to be most effective, select the strategies that children need to make sense of the texts that they're reading at specific points in their development.** It's essential to be flexible. Because strategies differ for each class and often for each child, a rigid and sequential approach will not be effective in meeting individual children's needs. And children learn best when instruction is at a level that presents new challenges, an issue directly related to grouping. (See Chapter 4.)

Teaching the Strategies

We have found that, overall, effective strategies instruction takes advantage of much of what is already known about effective instruction in general. It starts with teacher modeling and scaffolding—or building from students' known experiences to new skills and concepts—provides active guidance and opportunities for students to practice, and leads students to independence. Following are basic techniques for teaching the strategies.

1. **Modeling.** Think-aloud modeling is critical to strategy instruction. As you demonstrate how to figure out a difficult word or passage by using a particular strategy, say aloud what's going through your mind. It's best to start with one strategy and then gradually add and combine strategies, as children are ready. Be sure to use the correct terminology for the strategies as you model them. Emerging readers relish learning new "grown up" vocabulary, and—just as important—the correct language provides a natural bridge to later instruction at higher grade levels.

It's also important to take advantage of opportunities for impromptu lessons that arise naturally across the curriculum. Integrating and modeling strategy use in a variety of text formats across the disciplines clearly demonstrates how strategies can be applied in many contexts. For example, when you initiate a new topic for a science unit, introduce a factual book about it. Together with your students, *predict* what you'll discover about the topic and, after completing the book, *summarize* new facts learned.

2. **Practicing and Reviewing.** Students need opportunities to practice the strategy with their peers and independently. In addition, it's essential to review strategies students have already learned and practiced. Lots of practice and review insures that strategies become automatic, and enables the children to scaffold from a familiar strategy to a new one.

Tips for Teaching Strategies

◆ Systematically plan strategies into instruction.

◆ Model new strategies and "think aloud" as you use them.

◆ Make connections between new strategies and what the children already know.

◆ Apply strategies to different genres, across different subject areas.

◆ Start with one or two strategies, then gradually build your repertoire.

◆ Use the correct terms for strategies, even with emerging readers.

◆ Provide extended chunks of time each day for independent practice.

◆ Keep strategy groups flexible.

◆ Use a variety of grouping formats, including whole- and small-group instruction.

◆ Use complete, authentic pieces of text for modeling and independent practice.

◆ Keep records of individual student's strategy use.

◆ Provide opportunities for students to reread familiar texts to build fluency and automaticity.

◆ Integrate strategies throughout instruction, across the day.

Pairing students to read is one of the best ways to promote practice and review. After a story is read as a class, direct students to find a buddy and reread the story focusing on the strategies that they know. Have the children talk about the strategies with their buddies first, then share with the whole class. Together, you and the children can make a list of all of the class strategies used, emphasizing the entire group's knowledge and progress.

3. **Selecting texts.** It works best to use complete pieces of authentic texts when you model strategies. Disconnected and isolated passages don't allow for using a range of cues to figure out unknown words. "Decodable texts," which typically contain contrived sentences limited to selected word families, don't work either. For example, children can't really use text-level strategies to decode, "Pat the fat cat sat on a mat."

However, poems, class books, magazine articles, and storybooks all work very well for modeling and applying a rich array of strategies. Picture books are particularly successful. They hold students' attention and interest, and cover a wide range of topics and issues that can relate directly to themes you're studying in other content areas. For example, we've used books on the life cycle of trees to model strategies in focusing on important concepts. This approach offers a seamless transition into discussions related to a current science unit. You can also select stories simply because they are personal or class favorites. When children are engrossed in a beloved story, they are more motivated to use a variety of clues to find out what happens next.

When you select books to teach strategies, look for . . .

- complete pieces of literature
- well-written text
- vivid and clear illustrations
- engaging and believable characters
- personal or class favorites
- varied genre
- diverse authors and illustrators
- rich and natural vocabulary
- appropriate use of high-frequency words

- connections to current events
- connections to students' interests
- relationships to class themes or units
- links with students' backgrounds and experiences
- slightly advanced text for modeling and Read Alouds
- how strategies can be applied

It's also important to consider the type of strategy you want to model when you're selecting a text. Does the reader really need to use focusing to comprehend the text, or is *visualizing* a more appropriate choice? For instance, *Brown Bear* by Bill Martin, Jr. (Henry Holt, 1992) is a great book to use with young children to model how to check picture cues. The vibrant illustrations in the text provide young readers with exactly the support they need in figuring out the correct color and animal words. However, *Brown Bear* wouldn't be appropriate for modeling *analyzing* because it doesn't have a main story character, setting, or problem and solution. (Appendix 2 provides a list of all the children's books mentioned in this text with suggested strategies for each.)

Assessing Strategy Use

Keeping simple records of students' progress, based on many different observations in a variety of contexts, will help you plan for subsequent instruction. For example, individual Running Records (see Chapter 4) help provide specific information about how a child uses strategies to figure out unknown or difficult text. Anecdotal notes taken during whole-group instruction and children's independent time also yield useful information (see Chapter 5). Formatted checklists (see "Checking Up on Learning" below) are another good way to track children's progress across a grading period or over the school year. Reviewing the checklist will help you plan instruction and share specific information about a child's development with parents and caregivers. Reproducibles of the checklists shown in the "Checking Up on Learning" section are provided at the end of this chapter.

> **TEACHER TIP**
>
> When you find a book that is particularly effective in supporting a selected strategy, attach a library-card pocket inside and slip a note in it as a reminder. For texts that don't stay in the classroom permanently —such as school or community library books—create a simple database of "top hits" for each strategy.

CHECKING UP ON LEARNING

Observational Checklists

Careful observations using checklists during whole-group strategy lessons, one-on-one conferences, and informal paired reading reveal telling information about how children grow in using strategies over time. As the grading period progresses, you can quickly scan the checklists to see what strategies a particular child is using and what future instruction he or she needs. We use two types of checklist: a "Student Strategy Checklist," which pinpoints the needs of each child, and a "Classroom Strategy Checklist," which allows for comparing progress and planning for focused, small-group instruction.

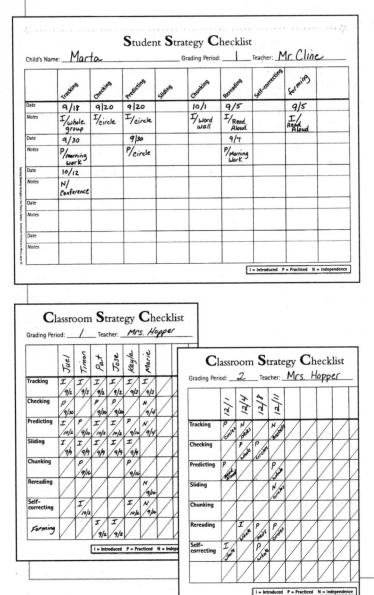

Student Strategy Checklist

The specific strategies shown here were chosen for a first-grade classroom. However, you can easily adapt or alter the list to target your students' levels. The purpose of this checklist is to provide a specific focus on individual progress throughout a grading period or the school year. It is an invaluable tool during parent conferences.

Classroom Strategy Checklist

This form provides two options for creating an overall picture of the class's progress. As indicated in the sample, one way to use the form is to illustrate a snapshot of the entire class and each child in it. The top spaces would be used to fill in each child's name. In the strategy boxes below, you would indicate the date and how the strategy was used (i.e., *Introduced*, *Practiced*, or *Independently*). The other way to use the classroom list is to fill in the date across the top and, in the spaces below, note whether that strategy is introduced, practiced, or used independently. Notations can also be made regarding the group structure of the lesson and the general level of comprehension of the strategy.

Classrooms That Support Strategic Reading

We've found that for effective strategies instruction a classroom environment embodies what is already known about creating a comfortable but exciting place to learn. A look at Melody's first-grade classroom, as seen through a strategies prism, can serve as an example. The classroom environment, both in terms of physical space and instructional content, can greatly influence the effectiveness of strategic reading instruction.

Classroom Environment

Decisions about such matters as where students sit, what special spaces are important, and how to schedule influence the effectiveness of strategy-based teaching and support.

Here are suggestions for planning classroom space and instructional tone:

Create areas that reflect developmentally appropriate instruction. For example, plan centers where children can explore and practice using strategies independently. In cozy nooks and crannies, include a range of texts and authentic materials such as maps, forms, grocery lists and newspapers. Provide a variety of writing tools as well as storytelling props and materials for drawing and painting.

Develop a strong classroom community. Establish a sense of community through clear-cut routines to give students a feeling of security, foster a sense of unity among students, and encourage interaction.

Schedule large chunks of time for instruction. Include direct, systematic teaching balanced with integrated themes and authentic reading materials.

Continually assess student progress and systematically plan instruction accordingly. It's critical to build assessment—both informal and formal—into the daily routine.

Make sure students are engaged in purposeful reading and writing every day!

Sources: Avery, 1993; IRA, 2000; Morrow, Tracey, Woo and Pressley, 1999; Novick, 1999/2000; Patton and Mercer, 1996.

The Physical Set-Up

When people enter Melody's classroom on any given day, they can easily see that it is a vibrant place that welcomes children and encourages them to read, write, and actively participate in their learning. The variety of student displays, colorful posters, and book collections placed around the room are carefully planned and organized to match the curriculum and student interests. Several aspects of the classroom arrangement strongly support effective strategic reading.

▲ Classroom libraries are natural gathering places to enjoy great books—and practice strategies.

☑ Space and Time to Explore Books

It's through independent reading that children can practice using strategies so that they become automatic. The easy-to-reach bookshelves in the carpeted reading corner give emerging readers easy access to reading. We often display author posters on the wall, along with a model of an alphabet tree from *Chicka Chicka Boom Boom* by Bill Martin, Jr. and John Archambault (Simon and Schuster, 1991), a book that is always a class favorite. The reading corner includes a wide range of books from wordless picture books to short chapter books to fit various ability levels. Class- and student-written books are also prized selections. By also including puppets and simple props for storytelling and dramatization, we invite young children to reenact favorite scenes or story characters.

Finally, reading nooks are not complete without a special chair to share stories. Decorating the class "Share Chair" can be an activity that involves parents and their children working together to make a unique contribution to the classroom environment (see Chapter 5).

☑ An Assortment of Writing Materials

As children practice strategies in their reading, they are reinforcing the strategies they'll use to decode and make meaning from the texts that they'll write. Therefore, a strategies-based classroom should include centers specifically for writing. Tubs of crayons and pencils, scrap paper for quick notes, bound draft books, and primary lined paper should be available to budding authors and artists.

☑ Spaces for Formal Instruction and Student Interaction

We suggest that tables be used instead of individual desks to encourage collaborative learning and peer sharing. Sitting at tables enables students to support each other in using strategies as they peer read or interact socially in grouped Book Clubs (see Chapter 4). Another benefit to using tables is that it saves floor space, opening up other areas for independent centers and small group instruction.

☑ Classroom Displays

Instructional and student-created visuals contribute to the learning climate that builds student confidence and supports strategic reading and writing. For example, we prominently display a large strategy chart and refer to it during whole- and small-group instruction (see Chapter 4). We also display reading buddy lists, poem charts, and book covers corresponding to the current author study. Displaying examples of *all* students' work also enhances the environment; highlighting work created by every child— not just those judged as "best"—encourages a sense of community.

The Instructional Context

Besides creating a *physical* environment conducive to a strategies-centered classroom, you also need to develop content that supports it in a rich instructional environment. Here are some of the techniques we use:

❂ **Themes.** Whenever possible, take advantage of seasonal topics, current events, or students' interests to build your lessons. By integrating themed content with strategic reading and writing activities, you provide students with the chance to practice their strategies with a variety of materials ranging from science and social studies texts to newspaper articles and Internet research. Consequently, strategies become part of students' daily learning and are readily transferable.

❂ **Student interaction.** With a classroom arrangement that encourages cooperation, students share tips as they are reading and writing together. Often, children are better able to explain how they are using strategies than adults can. They help one another figure out difficult words or make sense of a passage. A positive, cooperative environment encourages children to take risks and enables teachers to set high learning expectations for each child.

❂ **Many opportunities to read and write.** Access to literacy is, perhaps, the hallmark of an effective strategies-based learning environment. Therefore, it is critical that children have multiple opportunities throughout the day to read and be read to. Read to students at least four times each day. Include short, impromptu sessions during lesson transitions as well as longer planned lessons that are designed to model a specific strategy. Also expect children to read and write daily for a variety of purposes.

Teacher Self-Reflection

Because we recognize that meeting the needs of each new group of students requires continual self-reflection and the willingness to change, we developed self-assessment surveys to review our physical and instructional learning environments (see reproducibles at the end of the chapter). These quick assessments are based on what we've found to be the most critical elements of an effective learning environment.

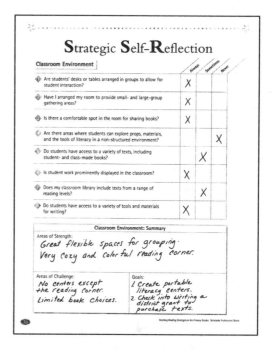

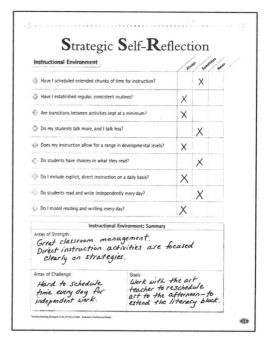

Strategies-Based Scheduling and Routines

Scheduling for a strategies-based classroom requires planning for extended blocks of time for instruction. Although interruptions, including special events, recess, and the little things that can pop up each day, are a natural part of the school day, teachers are often able to work with the school principal or specialists to insure that a fairly large chunk of uninterrupted time is available each morning for literacy instruction. A seamless block of instructional time, coupled with a variety of fast-paced activities that engage young children, supports an effective instructional environment.

Below are examples of what a morning literacy block might look like at the beginning, middle, and end of the school year. The actual day-to-day schedule will change in response to students' needs. For example, adjustments are made to the timing and type of activity as children develop their skills and as their attention span increases throughout the school year. Students might need an extended period of time to finish reading a favorite piece, for example, or the teacher might change the instruction to include a modeled think aloud when it is noticed that a certain strategy needs immediate reinforcement. This "planned spontaneity" helps teachers become more effective in their instruction.

SAMPLE SCHEDULE—BEGINNING-OF-YEAR

	Setting	Literacy Activities
8:00-8:15	Tables	Morning Work (Chapter 1)
8:15-8:20	Reading Corner	Read Aloud; word concepts (Chapter 5)
8:20-8:40	Reading Corner	Literature; whole group (Chapter 5)
8:40-9:05	Tables	Shoeboxes; traditional tale (Chapter 5)
9:05-9:15	Around the Room	Shoebox Pairs (Chapter 5)
9:15-9:25	Easel Area	Chart Story—writing
9:25-9:40	Tables	Draft Books—writing
9:40-9:45	Reading Corner	Author's Chair—writing
9:45-10:00		Recess
10:00-10:10	Reading Corner	Read Aloud; Big Book (Chapter 5)
10:10-10:25	Tables	Independent Reading; Book Baskets (Chapter 5)
10:25-10:30	Reading Corner	Story Share (Chapter 5)
10:30-10:45	Easel Area	Name Game (Chapter 2)
10:45-11:00	Easel Area and Tables	Notebook; Special Person (Chapter 2)

SAMPLE SCHEDULE—MID-YEAR

	Setting	Literacy Activities
8:00-8:15	*Tables*	Morning Work *(Chapter 1)*
8:15-8:25	*Tables*	Spelling; practice
8:25-8:45	*Reading Corner*	Literature; whole group *(Chapter 5)*
8:45-9:00	*Around the Room*	Centers; Strategy Circles *(Chapter 4)*
9:00-9:10	*Easel Area*	Chart Story—writing
9:10-9:30	*Tables*	Draft Books and Editing—writing
9:30-9:35	*Reading Corner*	Author's Chair—writing
9:35-9:45	*Tables*	Notebook; poem *(Chapter 5)*
9:45-10:00		Recess
10:00-10:10	*Reading Corner*	Read Aloud; Author Study *(Chapter 5)*
10:10-10:30	*Tables*	Independent Reading; Book Baskets *(Chapter 5)*
10:30-10:35	*Reading Corner*	Story Share *(Chapter 5)*
10:35-11:00	*Tables*	Word Wall *(Chapter 3)*

SAMPLE SCHEDULE—END-OF-YEAR

	Setting	Literacy Activities
8:00-8:15	*Tables*	Morning Work *(Chapter 1)*
8:15-8:25	*Tables*	Spelling; practice
8:25-8:35	*Tables*	Word Wall review *(Chapter 3)*
8:35-8:50	*Tables*	Word Tiles *(Chapter 3)*
8:50-9:05	*Around the Room*	Book Clubs *(Chapter 5)*
9:05-9:10	*Reading Corner*	Read Aloud; seasonal theme *(Chapter 5)*
9:10-9:30	*Tables*	Independent Reading; Book Crates *(Chapter 5)*
9:30-9:35	*Reading Corner*	Story Share; concept theme *(Chapter 5)*
9:35-9:45	*Tables*	Shoebox review *(Chapter 5)*
9:45-10:00		Recess
10:00-10:05	*Easel Area*	Chart Story; continuation—writing
10:05-10:30	*Tables*	Draft Books and Editing—writing
10:30-10:35	*Reading Corner*	Author's Chair—writing
10:35-11:00	*Around the Room*	Centers; Strategy Circles *(Chapter 4)*

Beginning-of-year: Initially, the variety of settings and grouping formats is especially helpful in maintaining young children's attention and actively involving them in their learning. Effective instruction at the beginning of the year includes:

◆ short activities with quick transitions.

◆ activities planned in various places around the classroom, so that children can have the opportunity to stretch and move.

◆ a variety of grouping formats (e.g., whole group in the reading corner, individual practice at their worktables, paired reading-buddy activities).

Mid-year: As the year progresses, adjustments are made to both the type and length of activities. For example:

◆ the Name Game is replaced with Word Wall activities that more appropriately provide practice with word-level strategies.

◆ Special Person and Shoebox activities are used as periodic review.

◆ centers are introduced, providing students with focused strategy lessons using texts at individual instructional levels.

◆ some activities, such as independent reading, are given more time as children's attention spans and independence grow.

End-of-year: Similar shifts are made to instruction toward the end of the year, in that

◆ Word Wall work becomes Word Wall review.

◆ other word-level activities, such as Word Tiles, become more sophisticated.

◆ Book Clubs and other small-group activities are incorporated to replace the previous emphasis on whole-group literature instruction.

◆ the time is extended for Strategy Circles.

◆ lots of time is provided for strategy review and for independent work so that children can practice using and applying the strategies in many contexts.

We have also included time for spelling and writing in each of the three sample schedules. Although not the focus of this particular book, spelling and writing integrate and apply most of the same strategies used in reading instruction. Through writing, strategy use "comes to life." Planning time each day for modeling and practicing both reading and writing is critical to young children's overall literacy success.

Managing Transitions

Transitions are particularly crucial at the beginning of the year. As all teachers of young children know, it's often difficult to get students' attention back on track once it has been lost! We suggest using the following techniques to ensure smooth transition times.

◆ Prepare all your materials the evening before and organize them in file folders or crates. This way you'll be able to focus on keeping your students' attention rather than having to search for mislaid materials. You'll feel relaxed and ready for the next day.

◆ Have a repertoire of transitional rhymes or chants on hand for those occasions when children begin to appear restless. For example, keep poster-sized copies of a selection of favorite chants or short poems on a portable easel. When you sense that the children's attention is waning, invite them to stand up and recite these familiar rhymes as you point at the words to reinforce the important strategy of *tracking*. Children can be encouraged to create movements and clapping patterns to go with the chants. You can use any short piece ranging from Mother Goose rhymes to rap pieces written by the children.

◆ Take a few minutes to have the children get up, stretch, and "get the wiggles out." This method will really pay off in the long run in terms of keeping the children focused.

Morning Routines

Consistent daily routines are an important element of strategies-based instruction. Children feel secure in knowing what's coming up, and thus feel confident enough to practice and share strategies. We plan our routines around clearly defined expectations for classroom behavior. Sharing books like *Never Spit on Your Shoes*, by Denys Cazet (Orchard, 1990), can provide a lively springboard for class discussions on appropriate behavior.

▲ Children enjoy sharing Big Books during their morning routines.

☑ Morning Work

As students arrive in the morning, they immediately go to their worktables to complete a variety of activities awaiting them. Melody selects activities that require little or no direction from her, allowing her to focus her attention on students who are arriving. Melody often joins children in the reading corner to share a favorite story as the remaining children complete their

Morning Work. On other days, she plays a story tape while a student takes the role of "teacher" pointing to the corresponding illustrations. Morning Work varies throughout the school year.

* In the fall, children can review concepts learned the previous year. First graders, for example, may review alphabetical order, counting, and color words. A review of sight words is quite effective for second or third graders.

* At the beginning of each month, children can also create and decorate folders that will house a variety of related work and themes for that month.

* Students can complete illustrations for Shoebox stories (see Chapter 5) or their own published books.

* Word Wall review activities are included later in the year.

* Extra challenge activities, such as generating rhyming words ("How many words can you write that rhyme with *cat*?") or filling in a number grid from one to 100, are also good Morning Work activities.

Morning Work Tips

◆ Avoid busywork; plan purposeful activities.
◆ Select activities that young children can complete with little or no teacher direction.
◆ Model new activities as a class before incorporating them into Morning Work.
◆ Focus on review of previous concepts; do not use Morning Work to introduce new skills.
◆ Provide choices, whenever possible.
◆ Vary the activities.
◆ Remember to include "Fun!" in the planning.

☑ Take-Home Folders

One of the Morning Routines in Melody's classroom involves Take-Home Folders. This system provides continual communication between the home and school. Each student has a folder that he or she takes home every day that is filled with homework, permission slips, lunch money, notes for caregivers, and so on. As the children bring back their folders the next school day, Melody welcomes them and reviews their folders. This personal contact at the beginning of the day makes each child feel special and brings him or her into the classroom community.

TEACHER TIP

As you check Take-Home Folders for returned homework, mark a simple class chart to show whether the work is complete (green dot) or missing (red dot). Organize any other materials, such as notes and lunch money, into separate piles for later reference. Alphabetize the folders as you check them in so that you can easily file papers to be returned home at the end of the day.

Here are some purposeful and fun activities that can be incorporated into your Morning Work routine.

Activity—Morning Message

Strategy used: cross-checking

One effective activity that can be used as part of Morning Work is the Morning Message. Morning Messages can be simple directions for the day's Morning Work, written on the board and should include the date, description of an activity the children are expected to complete, and alternatives to choose from when they are finished. You can also write the day's schedule and, as the activities are completed, the "daily helper" erases the list. This simple activity reinforces the strategy of *cross-checking*, as children reference the Word Wall and other classroom environmental print to read the message.

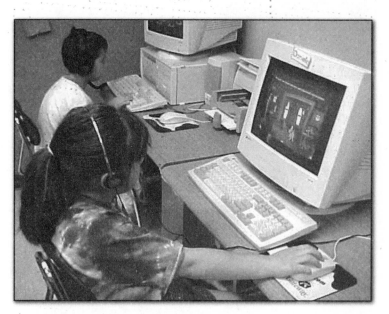

▲ **Access to technology will also enhance the strategies-focused classroom.**

Activity—Magic Wands

Strategies used: building fluency, cross-checking, forming, tracking

In a strategies-centered classroom, the independence that children gain from engaging in a variety of authentic and integrated activities is often clearly displayed when they pick up their "magic wands." Magic wands can be fly swatters, cat teasers, extra-long pencils, or actual wands from a costume prop box. The children use their wands in two ways:

1. **To provide the visual or kinesthetic reinforcement to help them focus on printed text.** When they have finished their Morning Work, children often gravitate to the jar of wands in the classroom and are "magically transformed" into confident readers. Some gather in a corner with a big book and take turns assuming the role of the teacher as they use the wand to *track* the print and *focus* on words they know. Others find a peer and a quiet corner and, together, use wands to reread a favorite tale chorally or follow along to a book on tape. While outwardly reinforcing students' use of *tracking* and *forming* strategies, these simple wands also reinforce young children's active engagement in text.

▲ "Reading the Room" is especially fun with magic wands.

2. To encourage children to explore the classroom's environmental print (see Chapter 2) by "reading the room." With wand in hand, children cross-check the room for familiar text to read and review. Bulletin boards, charts, enlarged poems, Word Walls (see Chapter 3), names, shelf labels, and the classroom calendar are a few of the resources children can use. As they discover text that they recognize, children tap the print with their wands and read the words or phrases as they build fluency with familiar text. While observing children as they "read the room," you can gain important insight into young readers' development in print concepts.

Morning Work Ideas

- Review concepts (color words, number sequence, sight words)
- Decorate seasonal folders
- Illustrate finished stories
- Travel on an environmental print "treasure hunt"
- Review Word Wall words
- Create Word Wall puzzles, word searches, word scrambles
- Read independently (free choice)

- Create story-summary posters
- Sequence story action with puppets
- Write captions for class photos
- Revisit favorite books
- Listen to stories on tape
- Write letters to school pen pals
- Critique favorite stories
- Chart favorite class books or authors
- Swap library books

By discussing routines and schedules and magic wands, this chapter has provided an overview of how strategies can be incorporated into effective literacy instruction. As strategies are modeled, shared, and practiced, you and your students collaboratively explore the world of literacy. Together, you'll use a variety of strategies as tools to unlock print through the careful selection of motivating and developmentally appropriate texts. In a strategy-based classroom, the tools for literacy independence are modeled, practiced, and provided to each child. This is a classroom that comes alive with the magic of literacy as seen through the eyes of self-directed readers and writers.

Letter Home

A STRATEGIES-BASED CLASSROOM

Dear Parents and Caregivers,

In the next few months, you will hear a lot about the strategies instruction in your child's classroom. Teaching strategies involves integrating thinking tools into reading and language arts lessons in ways that build on each child's talents and needs. This instruction uses practices that are developmentally appropriate for young children.

What is different about strategies instruction? The focus on strategies gives young children the tools they need to become successful independent readers and writers. The goal is always for the children to gain meaning and understanding from what they read.

What are strategies? Strategies are the thinking processes that occur in a reader's head when he or she is trying to figure out difficult text. Strategies include using picture clues, chunking together word parts to sound out words, tracking (following) the words, self-correcting, synthesizing, and summarizing. Different readers use different strategies at different times, and certain strategies work best in particular situations. Therefore, all readers need to be able to have a variety of strategies at their disposal—and know how to use them.

What is strategies instruction like? In order to learn to use strategies flexibly, children must be taught many different approaches. Usually we use complete pieces of literature, including great children's poems and picture books. We use newspapers and nonfiction books, too. Because learning is often a social process, children sometimes work collaboratively. However, there is always plenty of time for independent practice in reading and writing.

What might look different in a strategies-based classroom? A strategies-based classroom is easy to spot—it's the one full of books! You may hear your children talk about activities like Word Wall, Shoeboxes, Morning Message, Book Clubs, and Magic Wands. These activities are intended to build on known skills that reinforce new strategies for learning. All are flexible so that each child's needs can be met. And all build success and independence in young readers and writers!

Student Strategy Checklist

Child's Name: _____

Grading Period: _____   Teacher: _____

	Tracking	Checking	Predicting	Sliding	Chunking	Rereading	Self-correcting		
Date									
Notes									
Date									
Notes									
Date									
Notes									
Date									
Notes									
Date									
Notes									

I = Introduced   P = Practiced   N = Independence

Classroom Strategy Checklist

Grading Period: _____

Teacher: _____

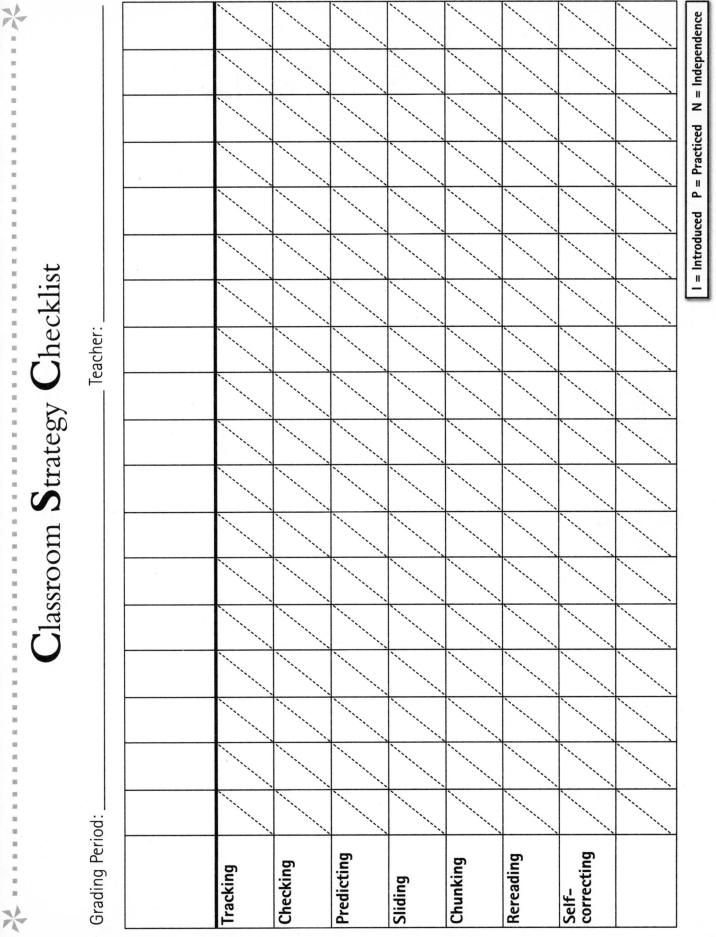

		Tracking	Checking	Predicting	Sliding	Chunking	Rereading	Self-correcting	

I = Introduced   P = Practiced   N = Independence

Strategic Self-Reflection

Classroom Environment

	Always	Sometimes	Never
1 Are students' desks or tables arranged in groups to allow for student interaction?			
2 Have I arranged my room to provide small- and large-group gathering areas?			
3 Is there a comfortable spot in the room for sharing books?			
4 Are there areas where students can explore props, materials, and the tools of literacy in a non-structured environment?			
5 Do students have access to a variety of texts, including student- and class-made books?			
6 Is student work prominently displayed in the classroom?			
7 Does my classroom library include texts from a range of reading levels?			
8 Do students have access to a variety of tools and materials for writing?			

Classroom Environment: Summary

Areas of Strength:

Areas of Challenge:

Goals:

Teaching Reading Strategies in the Primary Grades Scholastic Professional Books

Strategic Self-Reflection

Instructional Environment

	Always	Sometimes	Never
1 Have I scheduled extended chunks of time for instruction?			
2 Have I established regular, consistent routines?			
3 Are transitions between activities kept at a minimum?			
4 Do my students talk more, and I talk less?			
5 Does my instruction allow for a range in developmental levels?			
6 Do students have choices in what they read?			
7 Do I include explicit, direct instruction on a daily basis?			
8 Do students read and write independently *every* day?			
9 Do I model reading and writing *every* day?			

Instructional Environment: Summary

Areas of Strength:

Areas of Challenge:

Goals:

Chapter References

Avery, C. *And With a Light Touch: Learning About Reading, Writing, and Teaching with First Graders*. Portsmouth, NH: Heinemann, 1993.

Baumann, J. F., and Ivey, G. "Delicate Balances: Striving for Curricular and Instructional Equilibrium in a Second-Grade Literature/Strategy-Based Classroom." *Reading Research Quarterly*. 32, no. 3 (July/August/September, 1997): 244-275.

Block, C. C., and Graham, M. "Elementary Students as Co-Teachers and Co-Researchers: Methods of Increasing Strategic Reading Behavior." Paper presented at the Annual Meeting of the National Reading Conference, Charleston, SC, December 1993.

Fitzpatrick, J. *Strategies That Work: Helping Young Readers Develop Independent Reading Skills*. Cypress, CA: Creative Teaching, 1998.

International Reading Association. "Excellent Reading Teachers: A Position Statement of the International Reading Association." *The Reading Teacher*. 54, no. 2 (October, 2000): 235-240.

Morrow, L. M., Tracey, D. H., Woo, D. G., and Pressley, M. "Characteristics of Exemplary First-Grade Literacy Instruction." *The Reading Teacher*. 52, no. 5 (February, 1999): 462-476.

Novick, R. "Supporting Early Literacy Development: Doing Things With Words in The Real World." *Childhood Education*. 76, no. 2 (Winter, 1999/2000): 70-75.

Paris, S. G., Lipson, M. Y., and Wixson, K. K. "Becoming a Strategy Reader" in R. B. Ruddell, M. R. Ruddell, & H. Singer (Eds.), *Theoretical Models and Processes of Reading* (4th ed.), pp. 788-810. Newark, DE: International Reading Association, 1994.

Patton, M. M., and Mercer, J. "'Hey! Where's the Toys?' Play and Literacy in First Grade." *Childhood Education*. 73, no. 1 (Fall, 1996): 10-16.

Ross, E. P. "Teaching Strategic Reading." *Journal of Reading Education*. 24, no. 3 (Fall, 1999): 20-25.

CHAPTER TWO

Strategies–Based Classrooms

Special Places

> *In a supportive classroom environment, everyone is special.*

When children feel accepted and supported, they are more likely to participate fully and take risks as they emerge as confident young readers. In Chapter One we offered some definitions for strategies-based instruction and explored what an effective classroom might look like. In this chapter, we'll focus on one critical aspect of strategies instruction—the learning climate. In particular, we'll describe ways to focus on each child as a unique and special part of the learning community. The activities creatively integrate photos, children's names, environmental print, things that make each child special, cross-age buddies and the home-school connection.

Photos: Picturing Your Classroom

A great place to start to focus on individual children and to build a classroom community is with the children themselves—in pictures! On the first day of school, take a picture of each child with a digital camera. (If a digital camera isn't available, you can easily scan or digitize conventional film at department store photo counters.) Digital photos are flexible; you can easily replicate them and enlarge them. Your student photos will serve as a springboard for strategies instruction all year long.

With each photo activity you engage in, be sure to include labels for the children's names in bold, clear print. Names have a very special significance to young children (see "Name Activities" later in this chapter). Seeing their names with the photos also helps young children learn their classmates' names, which will facilitate the sense of community. And you can introduce the initial strategy lessons for *forming sounds* and *building fluency* as you and the children read familiar names.

The following activities illustrate how "pictures can tell a thousand words"— and help develop a class of readers!

✳ Photo Activities

Ways to Use Photos

- Classroom Community bulletin boards
- Open House invitations
- "All About Us" class books
- "Favorites" charts (e.g., favorite books, favorite playground equipment)
- Personalized bookmarks
- Seating or grouping assignments
- Class mobiles or montages
- Hallway or center passes
- Library sign-out
- Rebus-style stories or plays
- "About the Author" pages
- Photo/name matching activity
- Initial letter sorting
- Beginning/end of year comparisons

Activity—Photo Gallery

Strategies used: building fluency, forming sounds

Here are three ways to use photos of all the children in the class in Photo Galleries. You'll come up with others.

✳ **A bulletin board** made in the shape of a schoolhouse with the children's

photos and names inside

* **A border for the chalkboard** or bulletin board, made from enlarged photos

* **A mobile of photos,** hung from the ceiling

Students practice *forming sounds* and *building fluency* strategies as they read names. These familiar names and their sounds will also serve as references for students when attempting new words. And beginning-of-the-year activities—like having one or two students a day point to their photos, say their names, and tell something about themselves—will advance the sense of community, too.

Activity—I Can Read

Strategies used: building fluency, cross-checking

Create an "I-Can-Read" bulletin board. Place each child's photo on the bulletin board, titled *I Can Read*. Then, write the children's names on individual index cards and pass them out to the students. As each child says his or her name, they place their card on the board under their photo. Instantly, the entire class is transformed into readers! Although this is a simple activity, it reinforces the importance of *building fluency* and confidence in learning to read.

Activity—Class Book

Strategies used: building fluency, previewing

Create a class book by combining digital or scanned photos with children's dictated stories (reproducibles are provided at the end of the chapter). For example, each page might include a child's photo and a brief description of his or her favorite classroom or after-school activities. The children can also author their own texts (see reproducibles). Their individualized pages might include:

* favorite books
* favorite foods
* family portraits
* favorite animals
* pet photos
* descriptions of clubs and hobbies

Put the child's photo on the cover; subsequent pages can include photos from home or the child's own illustrations. These book formats help children become familiar with their classmates. As you share books with the class, model the strategy of *previewing* to overview the photos and text. As children reread the books independently, they *build fluency* while practicing early print concepts such as letter and word recognition.

Names: I Am Special

Integrating names into early literacy instruction builds children's confidence and helps them succeed. It also serves as a springboard into early strategies lessons by:

* ✳ enhancing visual discrimination

* ✳ developing letter knowledge

* ✳ developing initial-sound recognition

* ✳ emphasizing familiar text

* ✳ strengthening the relationship between oral and written language

* ✳ developing letter sequencing

* ✳ discriminating between upper- and lowercase letters

A number of children's books, including *Chrysanthemum* by Kevin Henkes (Mulberry, 1991), and *The Boy Who Would Not Say His Name* by Elizabeth Vreeken

What the Experts Say About . . .

Names

A child's own name is a powerful tool for literacy acquisition and learning. Even very young children have little difficulty recognizing their own name in print. Using names for instruction provides:

Recognition. Often children's first recognizable written words, names can be the "touchstone" for answering questions about written language.

Scaffolding. Names build an understanding of letters, words, and how they work. As children read and write names in a variety of contexts, instruction can support alphabet learning.

Personal literacies. Names allow children to establish their identities in written form and offer a tool for exploring literacy.

Connection to writing. Names have great impact on a child's writing development. Children often know "their letter" before any other, and can write their name before most other words.

Print resource. Children use their names, and the posted names of their classmates, as a resource for their reading and writing. They can use letter-sound knowledge gained from their names to read other words.

Assessment tool. Names provide insight into the development of a child's knowledge of letters. The letters children learn first are usually related to their own names, the names of people they know, or places in the environment they are familiar with. Young children see these letters as symbols that represent meaning.

Sources: Bloodgood, 1995; Fields and Spangler, 1995; McCarrier and Patacca, 1999; McGee and Richgels, 1989.

(Modern Curriculum Press, 1959), provide an excellent introduction to the topic of names. They're also great for the beginning of the year as you're getting to know the children and establishing a classroom community.

✳ Name Activities

Activity—Name Bulletin Board

Strategies used: sliding, stretching

Each day, post four to five blank sentence strips on the board. As you model how to stretch out letter sounds, write a child's name on each strip. Invite your students to count the letters and *slide* along from initial letter sounds. This is also a good opportunity to discuss the use of capital and lowercase letters. (For visual learners, cut out a name card around the shape of the letters so that its configuration can be easily identified.) Put the name cards up on the bulletin board. For reinforcement, write the name again on a second strip and cut it apart as the class spells out and chants each letter. Continue adding names to the "Name Bulletin Board" every day until the entire class is represented.

Variation:

◆ Put the cut strips in an envelope to use as part of a learning center puzzle activity.

CHECKING UP ON LEARNING ▶

Name Grid

One easy way to track young children's early concepts of print is to use large, bold print to create a reproducible chart for each child that lists the first names of all the students in your class.

In an initial screening of this assessment do the following:

1. Fill in the child's name on the chart and date it so you can record progress over time.

2. Ask the child to point out and read the letters on the chart. Circle correct responses. Write incorrect responses next to the letter.

3. Leave unknown letters unmarked.

For a more advanced screening, ask children to identify the names instead of individual letters.

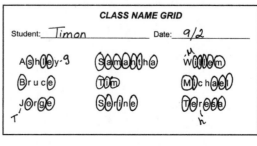

Activity—What We Wore

Strategies used: building fluency, checking

For this activity, use the children's book, *Mary Wore Her Red Dress and Henry Wore His Green Sneakers* by Merle Peek (Clarion Books, 1985). In the story, the clothes that animal guests wear to a child's birthday party are vividly accentuated by the text's illustrations—contrasting black and white with the colors as they are introduced.

After reading the book several times to explore the colors, have the children use a black marker or crayon to draw a large picture of themselves and then choose one article of clothing to paint a bright color (orange shirt, blue socks). Finally, print text across the bottom of the page, following the pattern of the book:

_____ (child's name) *wore her/his* _____ (color) _____ (article of clothing) *all day long.*

You can first post completed drawings in the hallway, and later bind them as a class Big Book the children can read throughout the year. The familiar patterned language and simple illustrations provide a perfect text for *building fluency* and for modeling the strategy of *checking* picture cues.

Activity—Alphabet Book

Strategies used: sliding, stretching

This collaborative text combines elements of classroom photos and children's names. Give each child his or her photo, which has been glued or scanned onto construction paper. Then, have the children use the first letter of their names to write a page for a class alphabet book. The text can be simple (*A is for Anita.*). Or, the children can write or dictate longer passages (*A is for Anita. Anita loves to eat chocolate.*) Focusing on initial letters is a great introduction to word-level strategies such as *sliding* and *stretching*.

As each child reads his or her completed passage to the class, help the class alphabetize the pages for the final product. The class book can also be duplicated and used as a Shoebox story (see Chapter 5) or taken home so that children can more quickly become familiar with their new classmates.

Name Games

The following ideas can extend name activities for a variety of contexts and learners.

Alphabetizing. Have children come to the front of the room with a large name card and put themselves in order alphabetically by simply keeping names together that begin with the same letter (*Sierra*, *Sam*, and *Sancho*). For more advanced learners, have students alphabetize within names that begin with the same letter (*Sam*, *Sancho*, and *Sierra*).

Name Sorts. Have beginners use large index cards and a pocket chart to sort names by initial letter. An activity for more advanced students focuses on other features of the names—vowel sounds, blends, chunks, or syllables. You can also ask students to suggest any additional patterns. These sorts often reveal interesting information about students' understanding of word-level and decoding concepts, such as the recognition that their classmates' names might also be the same as favorite storybook characters.

Class Alliteration Book. Have students expand on the idea of a name alphabet book through alliteration. For example, instead of a page reading simply, *C is for Carlos*, students could come up with *Carlos can continuously count coins*. This activity is particularly effective when children work in pairs or small groups to reate the text and accompanying illustrations. The resulting book of personalized tongue twisters and unique illustrations quickly becomes a classroom favorite.

Activity—Name Sorts

Strategies used: stretching, thinking aloud, tracking

This activity integrates students' names with early reading concepts. Give each child an index card with his or her name written on it in bold letters. As you *track* using the class alphabet chart, invite any child whose name begins with an A to come to the front of the class. As the children match the first letter of their names to the alphabet chart, have them group their "A" names together in a large pocket chart or on a central bulletin board. Continue through the alphabet, making sure to reinforce each initial sound. When the chart is completed, keep it in the classroom for reference in both reading and writing. Students may refer to the chart, for example, to remember what the /r/ sound is like (*R is for Rodriquez!*). This recognition leads to the word-level strategy of *stretching*, which you can model often as you *think aloud* through shared-reading activities.

Activity—Name Game

Strategies used: predicting, sliding, stretching,

A more advanced version of Name Sort, the Name Game reinforces all letters within the students' names. It's a good activity to incorporate at the beginning of the year to reinforce word-level or phonics concepts. Write each child's name in advance on large index cards and set them aside. Have the children gather in the reading corner around a large pocket chart and follow these six steps:

1. Announce the day's selected letter (C, for example).

2. Ask the children to *predict* whether there are more children whose name contains the letter *C* than there are without a *C*. Remind students to look for the focus letter anywhere within each name, not just at the beginning.

3. Call each child to the chart. Ask each to determine whether or not the selected letter is in his or her name and then place the name card either at the top of the chart (if it contains a *C*) or at the bottom (if it does not).

▲ Classmates are introduced to each other by playing the Name Game.

4. After all of the children's names are placed onto the pocket chart, have the students check their prediction to determine whether there are more or fewer names with the letter of the day (*C*) in them.

5. Have the class then cheer each name that contains this selected letter. And as the class cheers for Carlos, for example, they might simultaneously clap and shout, *C-A-R-L-O-S, CARLOS!* (See Chapter 3 for additional ideas on cheering). The cheering reinforces the lesson for more kinesthetic learners and engages all children in the activity.

6. Continue the Name Game the next day with a new letter, until the entire alphabet has been reviewed.

Variation:

◆ Use the Name Game to create a Letters-in-Our-Name book. Each day you play the Name Game, the class adds a new page to the book. This page incorporates the names of all the students that include the day's selected letter (**C**arlos, **C**athey, Sta**c**ey). Reread each page of the book to reinforce *stretching* and *sliding* and to review the names of all the children. This cumulative book grows as weeks go by until all the letters have been reviewed.

Name Game Scenario

Melody's students are seated on the floor around a large pocket chart. Melody announces, "Our letter of the day is C." She puts a large cutout of the letter C at the top of the pocket chart.

"Do you think there will be more or fewer names in this class that have a C in them?"

"More!" Sierra shouts. "Less!" others reply.

"Let's play the Name Game and find out." Melody takes the first name card from the stack. "Stacey, does your name have a C?"

Stacey nods, and comes to the front of the group. Melody hands Stacey a crayon, and Stacey circles the C in her name.

"That's right, Stacey. Your name has a C right in the middle. Good job, Stacey. Does your name card go on the top or bottom of the chart today?"

"It goes on the top!" Stacey answers.

"Why?"

"Because my name has a C."

Stacey takes her card and puts it at the top of the pocket chart. Next, Melody selects Carlos' card.

"Carlos, does your name have a C?"

"Yes!" Carlos retrieves his card, and circles the letter C.

"Why is the C in your name different from the C in Stacey's name?"

"Because it's a capital."

Melody asks, "Why does it have a capital?"

"Because my name starts with C!" Carlos puts his name card at the top of the chart, with Stacey's card.

"Next we have Brandon. Brandon, does your name have a C?"

Brandon answers, "No." Brandon takes his name card and puts it at the bottom of the pocket chart. "I bet I'll have a letter tomorrow!"

Timon jumps up and points to Brandon's name card. "Hey, Brandon has a *chunk*! He has the chunk *and*!"

"Very good, Timon. Can everyone see that? The chunk *and* is in the middle of Brandon's name. That chunk can help us read Brandon's long name. Let's all *stretch* this out together."

"BRANDON!"

"Excellent. Let's see whose name is next."

Environmental Print: It's Everywhere!

Environmental print provides another important resource for emerging readers and writers. Environmental print can be described as the text that surrounds us, such as:

- ◆ cereal boxes
- ◆ billboards
- ◆ calendars
- ◆ maps
- ◆ classroom labels
- ◆ traffic signs
- ◆ grocery lists
- ◆ posters

▲ Environmental print is a valuable resource in the strategies-based classroom.

Environmental print is usually accompanied by graphics that children can quickly recognize (for example, cereal brand logos or the specific shape of traffic signs). It would be impossible to escape the visual bombardment of environmental print!

Many educators feel that environmental print is one of the most effective tools used in an emergent literacy classroom because it is authentic and has a direct connection to children's lives. Melody says that Jill, her niece, was reading the *M* for "McDonalds" when she was just beginning to talk. All environmental text serves some kind of specific, real-world purpose that can have meaning to young children.

To capitalize on the effectiveness of environmental print, start the school year with activities that specifically incorporate this resource. Though emphasized early on, these activities also provide great review throughout the year.

✳ Environmental Print Activities

Activity—All Around Us

Strategies used: checking, chunking, cross-checking, previewing, sliding

Before school begins, collect print resources that are familiar to your students from businesses in your community—food containers, bags, placemats, drinking cups, and so on. Be sure to represent a variety of ethnic and cultural enterprises. Staple the objects directly to a large bulletin board entitled, "Look What We Can Read!" As new items are added, check the graphics or logos together with your students to determine where they are from. Focus on the first letter of each word,

Environmental Print

Reading labels, signs, and other kinds of accessible print contributes significantly to early literacy learning. Young children can read this print because there are enough external clues, such as specific shapes or graphics, or past experiences linked with these texts, to make sense of the messages they provide.

- Environmental print increases awareness of text. As young children become more aware of print and how adults use texts differently, they begin to realize that print symbolizes language and that these symbols hold important information.

- Most of what young children learn about written language comes from everyday experiences with print. Classroom instruction using environmental print builds upon what children already know about print and thus plays a critical role in literacy development.

- Environmental print can be incorporated in instruction. Teachers can include printed logos in class-created stories and label objects and signs. Students can also bring in examples of environmental print for a Community Box.

- Reading environmental print can provide an important context for learning about the alphabet and functions of written language.

Sources: Fields and Spangler, 1995; IRA, 1998; Kuby, Goodstaat-Killoran, and Aldridge, 1999; McGee and Richgels, 1989.

as you model how to slide to the end. As with the emphasis on student names, the focus of the environmental print board is on identifying initial print concepts.

Also encourage your students to bring print items from home, especially those objects that they can read independently. These might include restaurant menus, magazines, and newspaper ads. Spend time with each child's item, pointing out the initial sound and practicing the strategy of *sliding* to the end of the words. Then, add the item to the "Look What We Can Read" board (See "Send-Home Ideas" on the next page for additional activities).

Variations:

◆ Have the class decide on labels for each item (for example, *cup*, *carton*, and *box*). Print the labels on index cards and place these under the objects.

◆ Invite children to come to the board and identify individual words or letters that they "read" in the objects. This activity emphasizes emerging strategies involving *previewing* and *sliding* through to initial letter sounds.

◆ Later in the school year, use the environmental print bulletin board as a reference for other literacy activities. For example, when introducing the word *can* for the Word Wall (see Chapter 3), point out that *can* starts with the same letter and sound as the *cup* that is on the board. This demonstrates the strategy of *cross-checking* resources.

Environmental Print

Help parents and caregivers tap into children's natural motivation to read by giving them some simple environmental print activities that focus on strategies including *tracking* text, *checking* picture clues, and *accessing* prior knowledge and experiences. They can:

Create a "store" at home with empty food and product containers. Have the child pretend to be a store clerk, finding items for adult clients.

Create a book of favorite products, using logos for illustrations. Cut out logos and glue them onto separate pieces of construction paper. Have the child dictate the text for each page. For example, the child might state, "I like to eat at Burger House. I like to eat the fries." The completed book is bound using staples or yarn.

Go on a photo treasure hunt in the neighborhood. Take photos of familiar print such as stop signs, street markers, shop names, and so on. Categorize the photos (for example, all traffic signs) and then include them in a special Neighborhood Book.

Make simple concentration-type games using clean product logos cut from food containers. Cut out pairs of logos and glue each onto a separate index card. To play the game, lay out all the cards face down. The child selects two cards at a time, reads each logo, and decides if he or she has found a match. The game continues until all cards are matched.

Extend on the concentration game, by having children find pairs that contain the same beginning sound, or onset. For example, the logos for *Reeboks* and *Red Sox* would be paired as containing the same onset, /r/.

After the children have used the cereal boxes they brought in for reading practice, remove the top ends and use them as individual (and very economical) classroom mailboxes.

Activity—Cereal Box Reading

Strategies used: analyzing, building fluency

Cereal boxes are colorful, contain both textual and graphical information, and are usually geared specifically for the youngest consumers. To capitalize on the usefulness of this resource, ask your students to bring in an empty box of their favorite cereal (be sure to provide extra boxes for any child who doesn't have access to one). Have the children take turns sharing their boxes, identifying words or passages as they *build fluency* with familiar text. The class can also use selected boxes to analyze characters and setting as a very visual introduction to this strategy.

Special People: They Fill the Classroom

One of the most successful ways to develop a supportive classroom is to capitalize on the uniqueness of the class by celebrating each Special Person. Melody incorporates the following activities at the beginning of the year in part to help acquaint students with their classmates, but also to take advantage of the instructional value of using students' names as a vehicle for teaching. Melody initiates the activities using one Special Person as a model—herself.

❋ Special People Activities

At the start of the school year randomly choose a "Special Person" each week. Begin the Special Person activities with an interest inventory that the child takes home (see reproducible at the end of the chapter). Students and their families should provide information about their favorite books, activities, movies, and foods. Also encourage them to include items unique to their cultural or ethnic heritage, and to bring in family photos and a favorite book.

Use the information from the inventory and the photos to create a bulletin board showcasing the week's Special Person. At the beginning of the week, the Special Person reads through the items on the bulletin board and answers questions from classmates. Invite the child to read or "picture walk" his or her selected book. If possible, designate a shelf in the classroom library to house a copy of each child's favorite story.

Activity—Special Person Chart Activity

Strategies used: chunking, confirming, monitoring, rereading, self-correcting, stretching

To extend the Special Person activities create a chart story for each child. Incorporate these texts into students' notebooks (see Chapter 5) to provide an invaluable tool for strategy lessons. Convene the chart activity in the reading corner around an easel. Use the following steps:

1. **Write the Special Person's name on a sentence strip in bold, colorful letters.** The class cheers by clapping out the letters as the name is spelled. Focus on the name's initial letter and any *chunks* in the child's name.

TEACHER TIP

As part of the Special Person activities, have students create a half-page summary and critique of their favorite book and put it in the book as a bookmark. Younger readers can use a picture of a favorite story scene.

2. **Write the title of the story, "My Name is ____" at the top of the chart,** inserting the child's name.

3. **Invite the Special Person to share something unique** about him or herself that classmates might not already know. Write the new information on the chart, modeling how to use *stretching* and *chunking* to sound out difficult words. Also demonstrate how you *monitor* for understanding as the text is created and *self-correct* when an error is made.

4. ***Reread* the text with the class.** As you model how to use the strategy of confirming, make sure the text has captured the message intended by the Special Person.

5. **Invite the class to ask the Special Person any questions about him or herself.** Add the child's responses to the chart story. (We suggest asking students *not* to inquire about "best friends" to avoid hurting others' feelings).

6. **Reproduce the chart story for each child.** If a computer is available, you can reproduce the original chart story electronically via an LCD. Have the children *reread* the text with you as they follow along in their own copy.

7. **Capitalize on unique features of the text to reinforce strategies.** For example, ask the children to circle all of the proper nouns in the story, highlight sight words that have been previously reviewed, or underline ending punctuation. You can quickly adapt these mini-lessons to the class's abilities and to concepts you're currently focusing on in other activities.

8. **Finally, have students file the stories under the Special Person section of their notebooks** (see Chapter 5) for review and rereading at a later date.

▲ Special friendships are formed through learning together.

Cross-Age Buddies: They Help Each Other

It is Wednesday afternoon, and the first graders at Melody's school are down the hall in the fourth-grade classrooms. Pairs of students are in every corner and under every desk. Melody's first graders are elbow-to-elbow with their fourth grade buddies, bent over a picture book, sports magazine, or a variety of other reading materials. One pair suddenly bursts out laughing, as they share a particularly funny joke in a favorite

Reading Buddies

Pairing younger and older students can enhance the strategies-based instruction of all participants. All students increase their reading fluency, self-esteem, confidence, motivation, independence, and overall reading achievement.

Buddy activities foster students' capacity for learning in a cooperative context. They accelerate the progress of young children. They help older children develop leadership skills, a sense of responsibility, patience, and sensitivity. Older children also develop a richer repertoire of reading strategies, better inference skills, and an improved understanding of the complexities of the reading process.

Buddy programs work well for students of varied abilities and reading levels. Often, the older buddy is responsible for planning instruction for the younger child. At the conclusion of each session, hold a debriefing during which the pair discuss their experiences, reflect on observations, and plan for the next session.

Give careful consideration to pairing buddies. Research has shown that same-gender pairs are most effective. Be sensitive to abilities when pairing students. For example, pairing a highly fluent younger child with an older buddy who is struggling with reading would be ineffective and potentially embarrassing for the older child. It is also most beneficial to keep the same pairs together over the school year, in order to develop lasting bonds.

Sources: Brenno and Teaff, 1997; Chandler and Gibson, 1998; Fisette, 1996; Schneider and Barone, 1997.

riddle book. Another buddy team is poring over a book on stars, intent on finding some extraordinary facts to share with their respective classmates as part of a joint unit on the solar system. This is a Cross-Age Reading Buddies program.

A Reading Buddies program enhances students' literacy learning experiences across grade levels. You can integrate such programs across the school year either at regular intervals or during periodic special events. There are many advantages to cross-age partnerships.

☑ Preparing for Buddy Work

Careful planning insures that the buddy experience is rewarding for all participants and paves the way for a successful learning experiences. Here are three important planning tips:

1. **Find just the right location for the buddy encounters.** Depending on the type of activities planned, you can successfully adapt classrooms, common spaces, or outside performance areas.

2. **Before the buddy pairs meet, discuss routines and responsibilities.** It's sometimes intimidating for young children to work with older students. So tell the young readers exactly what they'll encounter in the Buddy Program. Have

the older buddies review techniques, such as holding a book so that the younger child can see the pictures, appropriate pacing, intonation, and questioning. A few role-playing sessions with their classmates can help ease the apprehensions of the older partners.

3. **Brainstorm how to behave with new friends and what rules to expect in another classroom.** Children need to consider things like: What level of noise is appropriate? What are the rules for bathroom breaks? Are there places that are "off limits" in the classroom (such as under the teacher's desk)?

☑ **Getting Acquainted**

After the buddies have had the opportunity to review expectations and strategies in their own classrooms, and perhaps to swap introductory notes or drawings, it's time for the big event! During the initial meeting, it's useful to have specific activities planned to break the ice. For example:

✳ You and a buddy teacher can begin by sharing favorite picture books or poems with the entire group.

✳ Student buddy pairs can meet to share their own favorite stories, which they've brought from home especially for this event.

✳ Buddy pairs can complete interest inventories. Try using the Special Person inventory sheet (included as a reproducible at the end of this chapter).

✳ These icebreaker activities help buddies get to know each other and are also helpful for planning subsequent lessons. For instance, when the buddies find that they both own dogs, sharing dog books would be a terrific way to start the next session!

✳ Buddy Activities

The initial get-acquainted event is also a great time to plan activities for future buddy sessions. For example, you might brainstorm a list of book-response projects such as:

◆ Story map pictures   ◆ Murals

◆ Book advertisements   ◆ Puppets

◆ Fact lists   ◆ Plays or skits

◆ New endings   ◆ Author comparisons

◆ Dioramas   ◆ Collection portfolios

Buddy pairs can then create their own lists and plan a project for subsequent sessions. In most partnerships, it is the older child who has this responsibility. However involving the younger buddy in this task can empower the young learner and reinforce his or her special place in the partnership! You can use a variety of activities to enhance the buddy-pair relationships and develop strategy use.

Expansions ◆◆◆◆◆◆◆◆◆◆◆◆◆◆◆◆◆

Buddy Lessons

Extending students' responsibility can easily enhance cross-age sessions. Once both classes are familiar with the session format and their buddies, the older students can begin planning the time together. One way to facilitate this new responsibility is to provide students with a form or template for the session (see sample; the reproducible is at the end of the chapter). You'll want to adapt this template to the needs of each group of buddies.

Before starting a lesson, have students review each other's plans and share suggestions for improvement. Peers can also practice reading their selected books to each other to build fluency and review the focus strategies.

Buddy Session Planner

Date: _10/1_ Book Title: _Three Little Javelinas_

Buddy 1: _Jill_ Buddy 2: _Dorothea_

Before the session:

What is the story/book about?
It's like "The Three Little Pigs," but takes place in the southwest.

What words will I need to review with my buddy before we read?
javelina, whirlwind, tumbleweed, coyote, saguaro

How will I introduce the book?
We'll talk about the story "The Three Little Pigs" and write 3 things we remember.

What reading format will I use?

_X_ read aloud   ___ choral read   ___ silent read

___ take turns   _X_ picture walk

What strategies will I focus on?
Checking the picture, predicting

What special project will we do after we read?
We'll write our own new version of the story.

What materials do I need?
Our Learning Logs, pencils

After the session:

What did I learn from this session?
My buddy has a great sense of humor!

What can I do better next time?
Practice reading some of the tricky words before I meet with my buddy.

Activities—Buddy Session Ideas

Strategies used: accessing, building fluency, summarizing

◆ **Build buddy sessions into your literacy instruction.** A regular schedule, such as meeting once a week for 20 minutes, provides continuity and reinforces the importance of this special partnership.

◆ **Encourage both buddies to bring a favorite story, poem, or article to each session.** The buddies can take turns reading the text. If time is a constraint, have the buddies share a favorite part in the text and *access* background information by taking a "picture walk" through the rest of the book.

◆ **Plan around a common theme, particularly when there is a unit that both classrooms are studying simultaneously.** Have the buddy pairs research the topic together. They might create a poster or presentation to summarize their findings and then share their research with the entire group.

◆ **Share Shoebox stories** (see Chapter 5) **or selections from a basal anthology.** These experiences provide the practice and review that is so critical for *building* fluency.

◆ **Share writing drafts or works in progress.** Buddies gain insightful critiques of their own writing as they edit with an authentic audience.

Activity—Chapter Books

Strategies used: accessing, analyzing, focusing, predicting, summarizing

Cross-age buddy experiences are ideal for introducing young children to longer texts that allow for extended conversations and the application of many text-level strategies. In preparation for the buddy session, have the older buddy choose a chapter book that is slightly below his or her own instructional level. This ensures that he or she will be able to read the book aloud fluently and that the concepts and vocabulary won't overwhelm the younger child. Have the older buddies practice their chosen books during their own independent reading periods.

Before the older student reads the practiced chapter book to the younger student during each buddy session, have the pairs *predict* what will happen based on illustrations or previous chapters they've read. They can also *access* their own experiences to make connections to the text. In order to *analyze* characters and story events over time, the buddies can conclude each session by illustrating an important event or describing a new character. These quick activities help both readers *focus* on important details in the text. When the book is completed, the buddies can *summarize* the story by:

✳ writing about and illustrating their favorite parts of the book

✳ creating posters as book advertisements

✳ developing a cartoon that traces the story's sequence

✳ writing a new ending

Integrate photos of the buddies into the final products and display them in the classroom or hall.

Home – School: The Connection Counts

Besides focusing on how each child is a Special Person and how, together, all students become part of a productive, supportive classroom community, a strategies-centered teacher recognizes each child is unique because of his or her experiences at home. We've developed activities that we call Chit Chats, which can replace conventional Show-and-Tell and encourage

TEACHER TIP

Chapter books that are particularly well suited to buddy sharing; include the *Junie B. Jones* series by Barbara Parks and the popular *Arthur* chapter books by Marc Brown.

interaction and communication, in addition to information sharing. Chit Chat activities can also forge the special home – school connection. By providing links between specific class lessons and home activities, Chit Chats enhance home- school communication and reinforce concepts being explored in class. In essence, several of the environmental print and Special Person activities described earlier are Chit Chat activities. Here are some other possibilities:

✳ Home – School Activities

Activities—Colors and Shapes

Strategies used: building fluency, cross-checking, rereading, sliding, stretching

Ask students to wear their favorite color to school as part of a unit on colors (parents can be invited to wear their favorite colors on that day, too!). On the appointed day, each child takes turns matching a color word card with the color he or she is wearing. Then, have students practice rereading and building fluency with these important color sight words. Students should also work together to determine a class favorite-color together and practice that color sight word as well.

Variations:

◆ Have children and their families find pictures of favorite foods to bring in for a class mural or to be used in planning balanced menus.

◆ During a unit on shapes, invite the children to find items at home that are triangular, cylindrical, or square. As children bring their items in to share with their classmates, you are creating a Shape Museum.

Activity—Family Interests

Strategies used: predicting, visualizing

Ask the children and their families to identify a small unbreakable (and non-valuable) item at home that represents something the family likes to do together (perhaps a stuffed bear to represent outdoor camping) and then come up with three to five clues to describe the item (brown, fuzzy, furry, soft). The children should bring their items to school— in paper bags so no one will see them. During a class Chit Chat share, each child takes a turn naming his or her clues while peers try to *predict* and *visualize* the bag's contents. When each item is finally revealed, the children have not only learned a little more about their classmates' interests, but have a new understanding of the authentic uses of descriptive language.

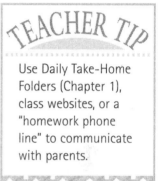

TEACHER TIP

Use Daily Take-Home Folders (Chapter 1), class websites, or a "homework phone line" to communicate with parents.

Activity—Language Patterns

Strategies used: chunking, sliding, stretching

You can relate Chit Chat activities directly to books you're reading in class. For example, after exploring the language pattern in *Silly Sally* by Audrey Wood (Harcourt, Brace, Jovanovich, 1992), ask students to work with family members to come up with another animal and something silly that it would do.

Silly-Sally Chit Chat

Greetings!

This week's Chit Chat activity is based on our class story, *Silly Sally*. As you will see in this wonderful book, the author uses rhyming pairs to describe the silly actions of animals (for example, a *loon* sings a *tune*, and a *sheep* falls *asleep*).

After reading this story at home tonight, come up with your own unique rhyming animal/action pairs. Remember, the animal needs to rhyme with its action. The rhymes will be shared during tomorrow's classroom Chit Chat.

Watch for a copy of our completed "Silly" class book later next week!

Have fun reading,

Mrs. Wolff

The challenge is to find an action that rhymes with the selected animal. Some of the pairs that students have created with their families include *goat/float*, *ape/escape*, *snake/bake*, *giraffe/laugh*, and *skunk/dunk*. Rhyming pairs provide a great way to focus on word-level strategies such as *chunking*, *sliding*, and *stretching*. Our classes collect these rhyming pairs and create their own modification of *Silly Sally*, complete with individualized (and often hilarious!) illustrations. In a follow-up Chit Chat activity, the children and their families reread their new books at home.

In a strategies-centered classroom, every child is celebrated for the uniqueness and special talents he or she brings to the class community. In this chapter, we offered a variety of ways to highlight how each child is special. We also introduced ways to communicate with families and bring them into the learning experiences of their children. Creating a learning community where every child feels special promotes interactions between peers and between the children and their teacher. And every child gains confidence as an emerging reader!

FOSTERING SUCCESS

Dear Parents and Caregivers,

Every child is a unique individual with different talents, abilities, and interests. Each child's abilities also develop at different times. For a classroom teacher, the challenge is to meet each child where he or she is at any given point in time and to develop a community of motivated and fluent readers who are truly "special" in their own ways. Using environmental print and name games are just two ways that adults can foster children's success at all developmental stages.

And what is environmental print? Environmental print includes the text and symbols that surround us—traffic signs, billboards, sports logos, and advertisements. Even very young children learn to recognize these symbols and "read" the signs to their favorite restaurant or the brand name of their favorite toy. Recognizing these familiar symbols is one of the first steps in learning to read.

How can environmental print be used to foster reading? In class, we may be using environmental print objects, such as cereal boxes, in a variety of activities to build the children's awareness that text contains meaning and in initial lessons on letter sounds. You can use this technique outside the classroom as well. For example, point out signs with your child as you go on walks or rides, and talk about the words and symbols. Go on a "treasure hunt" and see how many words you can collect. Read the back of cereal boxes, and create your own together.

What about names? Some of the first words that young children recognize are names. One way to capitalize on this knowledge is to create a scrapbook of names, including photos and simple text that tells about the special people in their lives. Don't forget the family pets! Use family names as characters in stories that you write together. As children read and reread these personalized tales, their confidence and success will flourish.

Class Photo Book Template

Our Favorite Activities

Cover page

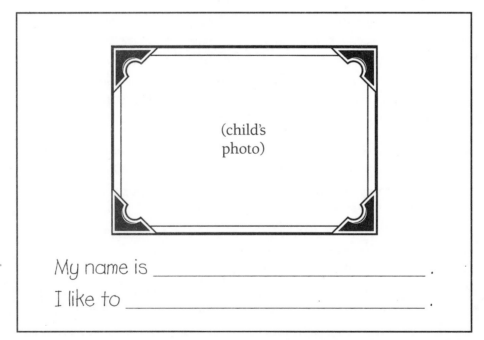

My name is _____ .

I like to _____ .

Page reproduced for each child

Teaching Reading Strategies in the Primary Grades Scholastic Professional Books

Student Photo Book Template

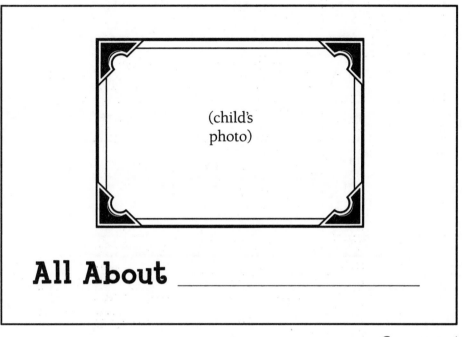

All About _____

Cover page

My favorite book is _____

_____ .

Sample first page

Family Members:

Pets:

Special Person:

Favorite Foods:

Favorite Sport:

Favorite Book:

Pastimes:

Collections:

We Are All Stars!

Teaching Reading Strategies in the Primary Grades Scholastic Professional Books

Buddy Session Planner

Date:_____ Book Title:_____

Buddy 1: _____ Buddy 2: _____

Before the session:

What is the story/book about?

What words will I need to review with my buddy before we read?

How will I introduce the book?

What reading format will I use?

___ read aloud   ___ choral read   ___ silent read

___ take turns   ___ picture walk

What strategies will I focus on?

What special project will we do after we read?

What materials do I need?

After the session:

What did I learn from this session?

What can I do better next time?

Chapter References

Bloodgood, J. W. "What's in a Name? The Role of Name Writing in Children's Literacy Acquisition." In K. A. Hinchman, D. J. Leu, and C. K. Kinzer (Eds.), *Perspectives on Literacy Research and Practice* (pp. 54-65). Chicago: National Reading Conference, 1995.

Brenno, J. and Teaff, T. "Big Buddy, Little Buddy." *Teaching PreK-8.* 28, no. 1 (September, 1997): 82-83.

Chandler, K., and Gibson, G. "Making Reading Partners an Integral Part of the Reading-Writing Curriculum." *The New England Reading Association Journal.* 34, no. 2 (Summer, 1998): 3-10.

Fields, M. V., and Spangler, K. L. *Let's Begin Reading Right: Developmentally Appropriate Beginning Literacy.* Columbus, OH: Prentice-Hall, 1995.

Fisette, D. "Tutoring Across the Ages." *Thrust for Educational Leadership.* 26, no. 1 (September, 1996): 34-37.

International Reading Association. "Learning to Read and Write: Developmentally Appropriate Practices for Young Children." *The Reading Teacher.* 52, no. 2 (October, 1998): 193-216.

Kuby, P., Goodstaat-Killoran, I., and Aldridge, J. "A Review of Research on Environmental Print." *Journal of Instructional Psychology.* 26, no. 3 (September, 1999): 173-182.

McCarrier, A., and Patacca, I. "Kindergarten Explorations of Letters, Sounds, and Words." In I. C. Fountas and G. S. Pinnell (Eds.), *Voices on Word Matters: Learning About Phonics and Spelling in the Literacy Classroom* (pp. 45-56). Portsmouth, NH: Heinemann, 1999.

McGee, L. M., and Richgels, D. J. "K is Kristen's: Learning the Alphabet from a Child's Perspective." *The Reading Teacher.* 43, no. 3 (December, 1989): 216-225.

Schneider, R. B., and Barone, D. "Cross-Age Tutoring." *Childhood Education.* 73, no. 3 (Spring, 1997): 136-143.

CHAPTER THREE

Integrating Word-Level Strategies

> *Good readers use many strategies to enjoy great books!*

The Reading Strategies chart presented in Chapter One (pages 10–11) summarized a variety of strategies to develop during early literacy instruction. Those strategies were designated as most appropriate for word-level instruction, text-level instruction (analyzing context and comprehension), or both. Although effective strategies-based instruction weaves both types of strategies together, this chapter focuses primarily on word-level strategies. Becoming a proficient "word crafter" helps children as they participate in Strategy Circles (Chapter 4) and engage in Shared Reading (Chapter 5). Some of the most effective word-level strategies include *chunking, sliding, stretching,* and *tracking* as a text is read.

This chapter also provides the framework for some very critical—and often controversial—issues in early literacy instruction such as phonics, sight words, and vocabulary. The study of words includes looking closely at sound-symbol relationships (phonics) as an aid to accurate and efficient word recognition. However, underlying all the topics we'll explore is the recognition that in order to become proficient in word study, children must be engaged in authentic reading activities every day.

What About Phonics?

So, what's the word on phonics? Is it really a necessary component in a strategies-centered literacy classroom? Many studies confirm that phonics is indeed an essential component of any early reading program. However, it is only one component, and it's not equally effective for all students. Some educators contend, for example, that an emphasis on phonics is only needed during the first half of the year to get children who enter school with limited reading experiences off to a

What the Experts Say About . . .

Phonics

Probably nothing has polarized reading education more than the debate on phonics instruction. All rhetoric aside, however, remaining is a core of beliefs most teachers can agree on:

Phonics knowledge is important in learning how to read and write, and most teachers incorporate phonics into their literacy instruction.

The ability to decode assists young learners in becoming independent readers; it also assists in their writing development.

Effective phonics instruction builds on a child's experiences with print, and should be integrated into a total literacy program—not taught separately.

To learn to decode the sounds and symbols of language, children need lots of experiences reading connected text. Matching oral language to print through dictation, tracking taped stories, singing, and chanting are all authentic literacy events.

Effective phonics instruction avoids the rote memorization of rules. Effective decoders see words not in terms of rules, but through patterns of letters and sounds.

Effective phonics instruction provides the tools that enable children to recognize words quickly. Therefore, children can turn their attention to making meaning from text.

Sources: Dahl and Scharer, 2000; Fields and Spangler, 1995; Juel and Minden-Cupp, 2000; Stahl, 1992; Stahl, Duffy-Hester, and Stahl, 1998

solid start. Children who enter school with some reading ability, they say, probably do not benefit as much from a phonics emphasis and instead progress much more quickly by being exposed to trade books and self-directed writing.

The primary issue in strategies-centered literacy instruction is not whether phonics should be taught, but how it should be integrated across the school day. Here are suggestions:

* **Provide students with a tooibox of strategies to use when encountering new words.** Demonstrate how to apply various strategies across different contexts.

* **Weave the thoughtful study of words and word parts throughout the day.** Focus on strategies that are clearly transferable to what the children are currently reading and writing.

* **Introduce phonics concepts at the point of use,** or when students most need that particular skill.

* **Incorporate a variety of assessments to determine what concepts are needed,** including writing samples, checklists, reading logs, observations, and Running Records (Chapter 4).

* **Provide instruction that is clear and direct.** Explain the new concept, and model it through authentic text.

* **Examine common patterns and similarities in words.** Because it would be impossible to teach directly all the letter-sound correspondences children would need to sound out each new word, select common patterns or chunks as a base for instruction.

* **Focus on onsets and rimes.** An *onset* is the part of syllable that comes before the vowel (*st-* in the word *stack*). The *rime* is the part of the syllable from the vowel onward (*-ack*).

Effective phonics instruction:	Ineffective phonics instruction:
◆ sustains a brisk pace	◆ dominates literacy instruction for all children
◆ matches what is read with concepts and strategies being taught	◆ emphasizes the memorization of rules
◆ engages children in activities that are relevant and purposeful	◆ emphasizes words in isolation
◆ includes writing as a significant component	◆ bases lessons on worksheets
◆ emphasizes chunks and patterns in words	◆ uses decodable texts as the primary resource in reading
◆ differentiates lessons based on individual children's needs	◆ takes up a lot of instructional time every day
◆ engages children in decision-making and hands-on activities	◆ extends a heavy emphasis on phonics beyond what children need
◆ exposes children to a variety of texts	◆ requires children to master phonics before learning to read
◆ integrates what is learned into a variety of authentic reading and writing tasks	

Teaching Word Study

Sight Words Are Significant

Crafting words includes not only decoding sounds and symbols, but also instantly recognizing the most common words in print. Interestingly, as few as ten words make up almost a quarter of the words in English texts. To read fluently, children must be able to instantly recognize and spell the most common sight words. However, sight words are often difficult for young children to conceptualize (How do you draw a picture-card to represent *of* or *the*?). In addition, sight words usually don't conform to common phonetic principles. Therefore, young children must use other strategies to learn these essential words. One of the most effective avenues is through repeated exposure to a variety of texts. Here are some other specific activities.

✴ Sight-Word Activities

Activity—Lightning and Star Words

Strategies used: cross-checking, rereading, tracking

Begin the school year by focusing on words children are already most familiar with. We've borrowed the term "Lightning Words" to describe the automaticity associated with these critical sight words (Cunningham, 1995). We display Lightning, or Star, words in large print on a prominent bulletin board or chart. As the students read and write together, we use this chart as a reference. For example, Melody uses a lot of poetry in her literacy instruction. While Melody and the students read the text aloud together, she *tracks* the poem with a Magic Wand. Then she gives students their own copy. They *reread* the poem, both as a whole class and in small groups or pairs, to build confidence and fluency. Finally, Melody directs her students' attention to the lightening words that reappear in the text of the poem. On their own poem copies, the children circle or trace over the words. Similarly, Melody models the strategy of cross-checking by pointing out lightening words as the class engages in Read Alouds, transcribes their Morning Message, or reviews the room's environmental print.

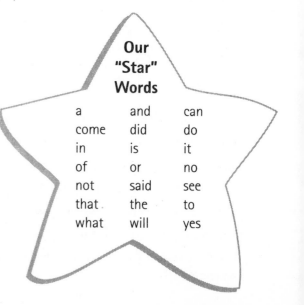

Our "Star" Words

a	and	can
come	did	do
in	is	it
of	or	no
not	said	see
that	the	to
what	will	yes

Variations:

◆ When you introduce a poem, have students match word strips to its text.

◆ Have the children create their own lightning-word cards to use as they Read the Room.

◆ Have the children take home a copy of the poem and their word cards for additional practice and reinforcement.

◆ Have the children find the lightning words in their own writing. As they work independently, watch for opportunities to have the children use the chart to *cross-check*.

◆ Model how you *think aloud* as you use the "star" word chart while composing a daily chart story.

◆ Create class versions of favorite stories to provide repeated exposure to common words.

Send-Home Ideas

Word Stalking

Give the children a list of the class's Star or Lightning words to take home. For very young learners, focus on only a few words at a time.

At home, together with family members, have children hunt for the list words in the print that surrounds them, circle the words, and bring them to class. Books, magazines, television guides, newspapers, letters, bus schedules, food containers, and junk mail are all full of sight words. (Remind children to ask for permission before they start marking up books and magazines.)

Create a chart or pictorial map to show all the places the words were found. Or have the class create a group list of their sources.

As an alternative, have the children and their caregivers tally the number of times that they find the targeted words in the print at home. Add each child's count to a class tally.

Activity—Fishing

Strategy used: building fluency

Students can "go fishing" to review important lightning words. Write pairs of the same words on index cards, and invite students to take turns fishing for a match. Each time a child draws a card, all the children repeat the word, *building fluency* as they review. Set successful matches aside or tape them onto a word chart. Make the activity more fun by cutting the cards into fish shapes and creating a fishing pole with a meter stick, string, and magnet. Attach a paper clip to the cards and have the children use the pole magnet to actually catch the fish word-cards from a plastic-bowl pool!

Word Walls Capture High-Frequency Words

One of the most prominent features in a strategies-centered classroom is the Word Wall. The words most frequently used in reading and writing are alphabetically listed on this large and colorful bulletin board. Our Word Wall is limited specifically to high frequency words. We make separate charts for vocabulary terms from class stories or units. The primary focus of our Word Wall is continued exposure to and practice with those words most critical to young students' reading and writing success. Word Walls that are made up of these sight words are beneficial for a number of reasons:

1. Word Walls help students develop a common bank, or dictionary, of words for their reading and writing.

2. Word Walls promote the awareness of conventional spelling. Once you post a word on the Word Wall, you can expect students to spell that word correctly across all literacy activities.

3. Word Walls provide emerging readers with constant exposure to those words that they will most frequently encounter in texts, and thus encourage children's independence as word crafters.

An example of a completed Word-Wall list is included at the end of this chapter. Keep in mind, however, that to be effective, a Word Wall must be based on a classroom's particular needs. Therefore, one class's Word Wall is not necessarily as effective for another group of learners.

☑ Developing the Word Wall

We've adopted ideas from Cunningham and her associates in setting up the Word Wall (Cunningham, 1995; Cunningham & Allington, 1999). Follow these simple guidelines:

* Introduce only a few words at a time (for example, five new words a week).

* Be selective; choose only those words that the class is currently using.

* Focus on high-frequency words. Other class charts can be created for story or unit vocabulary.

▲ The Word Wall is a focal point in a strategies-based classroom.

* Alphabetize the Word Wall in a natural progression from left to right to reinforce directionality. Also leave plenty of space below each letter for adding words throughout the year.

* Use bold, clear print. Make sure that children can read the word cards from anywhere in the room.

* To avoid confusion, match the font used in creating the Word Wall with the classroom's handwriting program.

* Because of potential problems with glare, do not laminate the word cards.

* Review the Word Wall words regularly and point them out throughout the day in a variety of literacy activities.

* Highlight or underline those words that will be most useful in decoding similar words. For example, underline the chunk *ight* in the common word *night* to help children read words such as *sight*, *flight*, and *bright*.

* Stop adding new words to the Word Wall during the final quarter of the school year to allow for extended study and review.

* Take advantage of using the Word Wall as an informal assessment tool.

CHECKING UP ON LEARNING

Word Wall Assessment

You can use your Word Wall in a variety of ways to assess the progress of the class and the individual children.

1. **Keep track of the words you have reviewed to insure that each is reinforced.** Jot down the words in a weekly planbook or check off each reviewed word on a master Word Wall list (a blank reproducible is provided at the end of this chapter).

2. **Create a Word Wall list for each child to check on individual progress.** As you observe children reading or writing independently, use the sheet to check off independent use of the Word Wall words (a blank reproducible is provided at the end of the chapter).

3. **Keep a file of all of the rhyming words that students generate during their extension activities.** The file can be used as a resource for future Word Wall sessions and also to track class progress and understanding of rhyming and word-pattern concepts.

Word Wall Checklist

Word Wall Word	Date Introduced	Date Reviewed
and	9/30	10/6
are	10/7	11/2
be	9/30	
big	9/30	10/12
came	10/7	
children	10/7	
could	11/2	
did	9/30	10/8
friend	11/2	

Individual Word Wall Checklist

Student's Name: Stacey

Word Wall Word	Independent Reading	Independent Writing
and	9/8	9/10
are	9/16	10/2
be	11/12	
big		
came	12/10	
children	9/17	10/2
could		
did	10/2	
friend		9/17

☑ Introducing Words

Word Wall activities are integrated into the daily routines of a strategies-focused classroom. There are many effective ways to introduce new words each week. We use the following sequence:

1. Before adding new words permanently to the Wall, emphasize them by placing them on a "New Words" chart next to the Wall.

2. Read the new words together, as you model how to track the text. Provide examples of the words in sentences.

3. Point out the words within the classroom's environmental print or in a story that you've just read aloud to the class.

4. Point out common *chunks* in the words, or those words that rhyme with a word already on the Word Wall. Encourage students to suggest additional patterns and analogies.

5. Invite the class to "cheer" their new word by clapping, snapping, and stomping each letter.

6. Have the class practice writing the new words, as you use the overhead to model. Ask the children to put a large dot under each letter they've written, spelling as they go. This reinforces one-to-one letter correspondence.

7. Next, have the children draw a box around the word, following its configuration. Discuss what the box looks like so they have a visual reference when they see the word again in text.

8. Finally, let children stand up and physically form each letter in the word. To form the word *and*, for example, the students scoot down low for the *a*, scoot again or bend over for the *n*, and then stand tall for the *d*. Now young readers have a physical link to the new word.

9. Repeat this process for each of the day's new words.

✳ Word Wall Activities

With every Word Wall activity, take the time to extend the lesson by pointing out particular word patterns. Focus on such word concepts as prefixes, suffixes, and blends. We use a variety of other interactive lessons throughout the week to reinforce Word Wall words.

Activity—Word Hunt

Strategies used: confirming, cross-checking

Word Hunt provides strategy practice in both letter recognition and the use of cross-checking context clues for comprehension.

1. On a sheet of paper, students should list the numbers one to five.

2. Provide a simple cue such as, "The word starts with *j*. The rabbit will _____." Students find the *j* list on the Word Wall, and then select the word that best fits the sentence.

3. Together, *confirm* whether the word is appropriate by reviewing the children's responses.

4. As the children find each of five words, the class snaps, claps, and cheers the list for some exuberant reinforcement! The children also enjoy using their fingers to trace the words in the air—or on their neighbor's backs.

▲ Extension activities are a fun and important part of the Word Wall learning experience.

Ways to Celebrate Words

Say each letter as you...
- ◆ Clap your hands
- ◆ Flap with your elbows
- ◆ Snap your fingers
- ◆ Stomp your feet
- ◆ Touch your toes
- ◆ Tap your shoulders
- ◆ Bend your knees
- ◆ Rub your belly
- ◆ Jump in the air

Say each letter...
- ◆ With a spooky voice
- ◆ Hooting like an owl
- ◆ With your nose plugged
- ◆ In a whisper
- ◆ Like a squeaky mouse
- ◆ Like a cowboy
- ◆ Loud and clear

Trace the letters...
- ◆ In the air
- ◆ On the desk
- ◆ On your arm
- ◆ Across your neighbor's back

Activity—Mystery Word

Strategies used: confirming, cross-checking, thinking aloud

One of the children's favorite Word Wall activities is the Mystery Word. It gives the children practice in using the Word Wall as a resource and chance to review word-level concepts. Here's how it goes:

1. First, select a word from the Wall and write it on an index card. Don't tell your students what it is.

2. Next provide clues so the children can guess the word. When you first use the activity, and there aren't many words on the Wall, give two clues. For example, you might say that the word begins with *T* and has four letters.

3. Model how you'd arrive at the answer by cross-checking the list of *T* words on the Word Wall and counting out the number of letters for each word. This models the *thinking-aloud* strategy and shows students that they can use more than one strategy to find the mystery word. Have students write down their guess.

4. When students are comfortable with this initial introduction to the Mystery Word and more words are on the Wall, you can make the game more challenging. Provide up to five clues for figuring out the selected word, and have students write down their guess after each clue (see sample lesson). Typically, the first clue is that the selected word is simply on the Word Wall, and the final clue uses the word in a sentence. Other clues focus on print concepts, such as number of letters and rime patterns. Each clue narrows the choices.

5. Often, young children have a difficult time with this process of elimination, even when they are reminded that they do not need to have deciphered the correct word until the final clue. Use the overhead to model each step of the activity using the *thinking-aloud* strategy to demonstrate your thought processes and how you *confirm* that the guesses are appropriate.

6. As you finish with each word, reveal the response on the index card and cheer the word together with you students.

Activity—Word Jar

Strategy used: cross-checking

Here's a Word Wall review activity our students love: Read the children's book, *Donavan's Word Jar* by Monalisa DeGross (HarperCollins, 1994). (In this tale, Donavan collects new words, figures out their meanings by *cross-checking* the resources around him, and adds them to his special jar. When he's collected so many words that his jar overflows, Donavan shares his words with others.)

Build on Donavan's story, by putting new Word Wall words into a special classroom jar. Then, during transitions, randomly pull out words and have the children read them chorally, using other Word Walls words to help decode the word if they are having trouble. As a class, cheer the new word. Have children volunteer to use them in a sentence or question.

Mystery Word

Melody's students are at their tables facing the Word Wall. She secretly selects a word from the Wall and writes it on an index card. She places it beside her, face down.

"Let's see if you can guess today's Mystery Word. First, write the numbers one to five on your paper."

Melody watches to make sure all of the students are ready.

"My first clue is, the Mystery Word is on the Word Wall."

"Aw," Cloe responds. "That's always the first clue!"

"Yes, it is. Now, write down any word. Are you ready for the next clue?"

"Yes!"

"The Mystery Word has four letters. Write down your guess."

The children scan the Wall, select another word, and write it next to the number two on their papers.

"Are you ready? Make sure your second guess has four letters! Here's the third clue. The Mystery Word starts with a *W*."

"Oh no, I had it wrong."

"That's OK, Mark. Just cross out what you had in number two and write your new guess for number three. Remember, you don't need to have it right until we get to the final clue."

Melody watches to see if the children have chosen a four-letter word beginning with a *W* for the third guess. She jots down Juel's name, who has written the three-letter word *was* as her guess.

"OK, here we go. The fourth clue is that the word has the vowel *A* in it. Remember the other clues, too!"

The children check the Wall for a four-letter word, beginning with a *W*, with the vowel *A*. "I've got it!" "Me, too!!"

"Hold on. There's one more clue. Are you ready? Write your next clue by the number five on your paper. Here's your clue, it's in a sentence. '___ (blank) will you bring for lunch tomorrow?'"

"It's what! I knew it!" several excited children explain.

"That's right!" Melody turns over her index card to show the word *what*. "Let's think about the clues. The first clue was that it was on the Word Wall. Sam, what word did you write down?"

"I wrote down *to*, but it was wrong."

"That's OK. *To* is on the Word Wall. But remember, the second clue was that it had four letters."

Word Wall Review

The Word Wall provides a primary focus of word study in a strategies-based literacy classroom. Reinforcement at home will assist young readers in recognizing these important words automatically and fluently. Here are two techniques:

* **Create Word Wall folders for students to take home each week.** Simply list all of the year's anticipated Word Wall words alphabetically on two sheets of paper and glue them inside a manila file folder. (See sample reproducible at the end of this chapter.) On Monday, have the children use a highlighter to mark the week's new words and take their folders home. Ask them to practice reading the words in isolation, in storybooks, and through environmental print. Encourage them to have their families help them use the highlighted words in sentences and discuss their meanings. The following Monday have them bring back their folders—ready for highlighting the next group of words.

* **Create a cumulative list format for the take-home folders.** During the first week of Word Wall study, have the children each take home a sheet with only that week's focus words stapled into a durable folder. The following week, staple a new sheet of that week's words over the former week's list. By the end of the year, children and their families can very concretely track progress through the stack of Word Wall lists. The final sheet includes all of the Word Wall terms for the year.

TEACHER TIP

Portable Word Walls are an invaluable resource for children with learning disabilities or for non-native English speakers. Share the Word Wall with special teachers along with suggestions for the Wall's use.

Rhymes: There Are Lots of Reasons

Using rhymes in word study capitalizes on what children already know and takes advantage of the fun of repeating phrases and rhythms. Activities that focus on rhymes are perfect reinforcing word-level strategies such as *chunking*, *sliding*, and *stretching*. When you integrate rhyme activities, you're also exposing children to authentic—and enjoyable—experiences with phonics!

✳ Rhyme Activities ▶

Activity—Rhyme Time

Strategies used: confirming, cross-checking

Rhyme Time is similar to Word Hunt (page 66) in that it focuses on familiar patterns in words. Instead of using sentences as a contextual clue, call out a rhyme. For example, you might prompt the children, "Begins with *l* and rhymes with *bike* (*like*)," or "Begins with *i* and rhymes with *pin* (*in*)." Each of the target words for this activity must appear on the Word Wall. As in the Word Hunt, children *cross-check* using the Word Wall and write down each of their guesses as they *monitor* their progress. The class then reads and cheers the completed list together.

Teachable Moments with Rhymes

The Rhyme Time activity provides lots of opportunities to discuss various word concepts at exactly the time that children are ready to learn them.

Lower/Upper Case. When generating a list for the chunk *ook* during one lesson, Melody's students offered both *brook* and *Brooke*, which gave Melody the chance to discuss the use of capitals for proper nouns.

New Terminology. During that same lesson, one student suggested the word *rook*, which his classmates declared was a nonsense word. Melody suggested that she might have heard this unfamiliar word before, too, and modeled how to use the class dictionary to look it up.

Homonyms. When the children were generating a list of words using the rime *-ill*, one student suggested the word *bill*, as in the term *paying a bill*. Another student noted that ducks have *bills*, too, but they are different. Melody wrote *bill* on the board a second time. Then a student volunteered *dollar bill*, and Melody wrote *bill* once again. After drawing quick sketches of an envelope, a duck, and a dollar next to the three words, she briefly discussed the importance of using the strategy of *monitoring* to figure out which word meaning is being used.

Variations

The Rhyme Time activity also provides an excellent opportunity to focus on chunks or rimes, through extension lessons, giving students a chance to transfer what they're learning about word patterns and sounds to new words.

◆ For example, after completing the Rhyme Time activity, you might write the word *pin* on the board or on butcher paper. Then underline the chunk *in* and ask the students if they can think of other words that end with this chunk (*fin, tin, chin, win, thin, begin*). Reinforce the children's knowledge of spelling patterns by asking a volunteer how to spell each suggested word, before you write it. Other useful rimes are listed at right:

Basic Rimes			
-ack	-ad	-ade	-ail
-ain	-ake	-all	-an
-ank	-ap	-at	-ay
-ed	-ell	-est	-ice
-ick	-ide	-ight	-ill
-in	-ind	-ing	-ink
-ip	-it	-ock	-old
-op	-ore	-ot	-ug
-ump	-un	-ut	-y

◆ As a Chit Chat activity (see pages 50–52), ask students to add to the Rhyme Time Hunt list at home and bring back their responses. Then create a comprehensive class-compiled chart.

◆ Suggest unfamiliar words with the same pattern, such as *kin* and *shin*, and ask the students to try reading them. This tells you whether the students can transfer the chunk in to an unfamiliar context. It also provides a quick vocabulary lesson.

Activity—Rhymes in Context

Strategies used: chunking, sliding

Focus on rhymes as you and your students read stories.

1. **Select a book that includes many rhyming pairs.** Books by Dr. Seuss are great!

2. **After children are familiar with the story, invite them to listen specifically for rhymes as you reread.** With books with lots of rhymes, such as *One Fish, Two Fish* (Random House, 1960), select only a portion of the text so that students won't be overwhelmed.

3. **After reading the selected text, ask volunteers to name rhyming pairs that appear in the book.** Write their suggestions on index cards.

4. **Explore the patterns in the rhyming words and sort them into groups.** Model how to *slide to the end of the word* or identify *chunks* to decode the rhymes.

Variations:

◆ Ask students to suggest additional words that rhyme with those in the story.

◆ Reread the text and invite the children to clap or snap when they hear a rhyming pair.

◆ Give each student one of the rhyming index cards to hold up when their word is read.

▲ Contextual rhyme activities apply word strategies to text.

Activity—Rhyming Word Patterns

Strategy used: chunking

Sorting rhymes focuses young readers on word patterns. For example, the book *One Fish, Two Fish* contains the following rhymes:

* ✳ star, car   ✳ four, more
* ✳ sad, glad, bad, dad   ✳ go, slow
* ✳ run, fun, sun

    At the beginning of the year, or with younger learners, focus on the first three rhyming sets, which contain regular word patterns. Model how to *chunk* common patterns. Address the pairs *four/more* and *go/slow* towards the end of the year or with children who can use and understand alternate spellings. This introduces children to more complex patterns and helps debunk the common misperception that rhyming words are always spelled alike.

To save time, prepare rhyming word cards prior to your lesson. Put them in the book they go with. Or put them in a card pocket created by gluing half of a manila envelope onto the inside of the book's front cover.

Themes: Vocabulary Builders

What about words related to the class theme? Shouldn't they be included on the Word Wall, too? Because the primary purpose of our Word Walls and Lightning Words is to reinforce high-frequency words, we don't find it useful to include unit- or story-related vocabulary on these displays. They do have a place in our classroom, however, and have their own charts and activities because they:

◆ are of high interest to children

◆ deepen vocabulary knowledge

◆ provide the foundation for learning about new concepts

    The following kinds of charts serve as a reference during reading and writing activities and are perfect for lessons in word-level strategy use.

Concept charts. Some of the Theme-Builder charts we introduce to young children early in the year incorporate concepts related to numbers and colors. For example, we create a border out of the number words from 1 to 20 on a piece of poster paper. Similarly, we make a display with common color words. Other concept charts might include:

✳ Parts of Speech

✳ Rhymes

✳ Location Words (up, down, in, out)

✳ Directional Words (right, left, north, south)

✳ Basic Shapes (circle, square, triangle, rectangle, oval, diamond)

Unit charts. Strategies-based instruction often integrates units of study across the

Keep the Theme-Building charts posted to use throughout the year as classroom resources. To fit them in, hang the charts from previous units from an easel in the reading corner. Children might use them for reference during a writing session or as part of a Reading-the-Room activity. Type up individual word lists for each child to add to his or her notebook (see Chapter 5) or take home. You can also bind the lists monthly into a *Look At All the Words We Know!* class book.

school day. You can incorporate words related to units or themes in a variety of ways.

◆ **Family words.** Young students like to learn words associated with families (*mother, father, sister, brother, grandmother, grandfather, house*). As they come up with these important words, transcribe them onto a large, body-shaped chart.

◆ **Seasonal words.** Have the class generate cumulative seasonal word charts. In the fall, for example, put terms related to autumn on a large paper pumpkin and display it beside the Word Wall. Have the children add words to the pumpkin as the season progresses.

◆ **Content charts.** Theme charts often reflect terms from science or social studies units. When studying space, for example, have the children create a list of new words on a planet-shaped chart. As they read stories and articles, invite them to suggest new terms to add to their planet. They can include unfamiliar vocabulary, which they investigate together using a dictionary, resource books, or an electronic encyclopedia.

◆ **Author charts.** Similarly, chart words they discover through an author study. Encourage the children to refer to these as the study continues, and they'll notice that many authors use similar themes, characters, or terms across their writing. We've seen that young children particularly enjoy books that incorporate such favorite characters as *Clifford* (Scholastic, 1963, 1980), *Frog and Toad* (HarperCollins, 1970, 1972, 1979), and *Henry and Mudge* (Aladdin, 1989, 1997, 1998). Draw commonalities between these theme words and those on the Word Wall. Which words rhyme? Which have the same pattern? Begin or end the same way? With activities like these, the children are continually practicing a variety of word-level strategies and making connections between the Word-Wall words that are already familiar to them and new words they see in print.

✳ Theme-Based Activities

Activity—Word Riddle

Strategies used: focusing, synthesizing

As you develop a theme, write unit-related terms on large index cards. Print terms from each theme in a specific color, and use a different color for each theme. Once the children are familiar with the terms, have them try to stump each other through a collaborative game of Word Riddle. Here's how it goes:

1. A volunteer comes to the front of the room and, without looking, selects an index card.

2. He or she shows the card to the class. (Make sure the volunteer doesn't peek!)

3. The class provides the volunteer with clues to the word's definition. For example, the clue "it takes astronauts into space" might be given for the word *shuttle*. This provides practice with the strategy of *focusing* on important information.

4. As an alternative, the class attempts to pantomime the meaning of the word.

5. The volunteer *synthesizes* all of the clues and guesses the word.

When the class is through with a theme, tape the index cards along the wall. By the end of the year, the color-coded cards will encircle the room. Students can see concretely how their vocabulary is growing. Because children often return to a familiar topic in their self-selected writing, the cumulative list also provides a useful visual reference.

Activity—Board Games

Strategies used: building fluency, synthesizing

You can adapt most board games to use with selected Word Wall or Theme-Builder words by incorporating Word Wall cards instead of using existing game cards. For example, to move forward on the board, students must first draw a card, read the word, and use it in a sentence.

Variation:

◆ Encourage children to create their own game boards. When studying a unit on gardens, for example, students can make their own colorful board with illustrations of flowers, seeds, trees, and tools, thereby *synthesizing* information they've learned in the unit.

Word Tiles: They're Interactive

One of the most effective word-study lessons involves manipulating Word Tiles to explore patterns in words. You can easily make Word Tiles (see suggestions provided). They are simply sets (one for each child) of individual letters—one for each letter of the alphabet. Word-Tile activities are especially good for young learners because each child is involved with creating his or her own words. Interactive experiences with the tiles that focus on patterns provide young children with a deeper understanding of the relationships between letters and sounds.

▲ Word Tiles actively engage young learners

◆ Cut tag board into approximately one-inch squares for the tiles.

◆ Print letters in a very bold font.

◆ Laminate the tiles to insure longevity.

◆ Print vowels in a contrasting color.

◆ Print the capital for each letter on the reverse of the tile.

◆ Store individual tiles in a small plastic hardware case with compartments to organize them.

◆ Create a large Word Tile set (large enough to slip into a pocket chart) for the classroom.

✳ Word Tile Activities

Activity—Making Words

Strategies used: chunking, sliding, stretching

We've found the Making Words activity to be particularly successful in modeling and reinforcing a variety of word-level strategies (Cunningham & Hall, 1994). As words are made, the focus is on one or two patterns at a time. Use and modify the following steps as your students "make words."

1. Give each student a set of selected tiles (for example, the letters *c, e, h, i, k, n,* and *t*).

2. Place a corresponding set of large tiles at the bottom of a classroom pocket chart.

3. Call out simple words. ("Make the word *it*.")

4. The children use their Word Tiles to make the word.

5. Have a volunteer spell the word out loud and recreate it in the pocket chart.

6. Go on to the next word ("Now make *hit*." You're building on the rime *it*).

7. End the lesson ends with a "mystery word" that uses all of the letter tiles (*thicken*).

8. Have the children alphabetize their Word Tile set and return the tiles to the organizer.

This example session of the Making Words lesson sequence shows how Word Tile activities provide concrete experiences in *chunking, sliding,* and *stretching* rimes, (*-it, -ick*) and onsets (*sl-, st-*).

Word Tiles—Example Session

Letter Tiles: *c, e, h, i, k, n, t*

    Start with two tiles and make *it*.

    Add one tile, and make *hit*.

    Change one tile, and make *kit*.

    Add one tile, and make *kite*.

    Change the ending (rime), and make *kin*.

    Take away one tile, and make *in*.

    Add one tile, and make *tin*.

    Change the rime, and make *tick*.

    Add one tile, and make *thick*.

    Change the beginning (onset), and make *Nick* (note the capital)

    Change the onset, and make *hick*.

    Change the rime, and make *hint*.

Other possible words: *hitch, nitch, the, then, hen, ten, Ken, chin, chink, think, ink, ice, nice*

Onsets/blends: *ch-, th-*

Rimes: *-it, -ick, -itch, -in, -ink, -ite, -int, -ice, -en*

Extended lesson: adding suffix *-en*

Mystery word: *thicken*

Activity—Analogies

Strategies used: building fluency, chunking

One of the most important steps in the Word-Tile lessons is to focus on analogies, or word patterns. As each new word is created in the Making-Words activity, write it on an index card (or use a prepared set of words), and put the card at the top of a pocket chart. When you've included all of the focus words, have the class reread the list of words, *building* their *fluency* and confidence. Then ask them to sort the words in one of the following ways:

◆ Categorize words into groups such as *hit*, *sit*, and *kit*, *knit*. Ask students to use such strategies as *chunking* to determine how the words are the same (word patterns).

◆ Generate additional words (say *lit*, *bit*), that

▲ Word Tiles activities reinforce many word-level strategies.

could fit into a stated pattern. Write them on the board for visual reference.

◆ Invite children to suggest their own patterns. This helps you find out whether they're recognizing word analogies independently.

Sorting words is a powerful activity because it focuses on word patterns and actively engages children's reasoning and decision-making. Besides common rimes, word sorts can also focus on word patterns or rules, vowel sounds, or even concepts such as verbs, theme-related terms, and people. The more actively the children can be involved in discovering different ways to sort words, the more strategic they will become. (See "Expansions" for ideas on expanding Word-Tile activities. Additional related professional resources are included in Appendix 3.)

Expansions ◆◆◆◆◆◆◆◆◆◆◆◆◆◆◆◆◆◆◆◆

Word Crafting

Here are some ideas for extending Word-Tile and sorting activities.

After children have had several experiences with Word-Tile lessons, encourage them to discover words themselves. For instance, provide each child with a certain selection of Word Tiles (not the entire alphabet). The number of tiles depends on the child's developmental stage. Invite the children to work independently or in pairs to create and list as many words as possible. Then, compile students' words into a class list.

Incorporate a discovering-words activity into a learning center. In the center, provide a set of five to ten Word Tiles and a chart to record words. Children can either create a chart independently or develop a large cumulative class chart.

Integrate Word Tiles into Chit-Chat activities. Have students use large grid paper to create their own set of tiles. Send the sets home with directions to use them to create as many words as possible. Compile students' responses into a class list.

After a Word-Tile lesson, have students use index cards or sticky notes to create their own word cards. Students will then work in pairs or small teams to sort the words into as many categories as possible and later share their sorts with the class. Have the students explain why the words are grouped together.

Encourage students to use their Word Tiles or word cards to create their own games. You might suggest versions of popular games, such as Concentration and Scrabble, but challenge the children to use their imaginations to create new game formats.

In the Game

One reason that Word-Tile activities are so successful is their game-like quality. Created appropriately, games can enhance a strategies-based learning environment by:

◆ drawing attention to phonetic concepts

◆ engaging students in thinking and problem-solving

◆ reinforcing word patterns

◆ developing rapid recognition to distinguish among similar words.

You can take advantage of students' natural enthusiasm for games, by building lots of word-level activities into them. Quick adaptations of common games can be very effective in reinforcing a variety of word strategies and in building fluency through repetition and review.

✳ Game Activities

Activity—Wordo

Strategies used: building fluency, cross-checking

Wordo (Bingo) is a particular favorite with our students. Create blank Wordo sheets that include handwriting guide rules (see the reproducible at the end of this chapter). You can laminate the sheets for reuse, or make paper copies for students to take home for practice. Playing Wordo is a great way for students to practice Word Wall words.

To prepare for the game:

1. Select the words you want to use. (Generally, you will limit the number of words and will repeat some words more than once on a Wordo sheet. Later, when your Word Wall has many words and your learners are familiar with them and confident, you might include more words).

2. Using the overhead, model how to fill in a blank sheet, writing the words selected onto the squares in random order. When appropriate, point out patterns in the words. (Also create corresponding word cards on index cards to use when playing the game.)

3. Before writing each word onto their own blank Wordo sheets, have the children snap, clap, and cheer it. Remind the children to vary the spaces they select to write the word on so that everyone's card is unique.

Then play the game:

1. When the children's Wordo sheets are filled, begin the game by

TEACHER TIP

To organize and save time, color code the Wordo sheets. For example, write your index word cards in red and ask students to put a red dot on the top of their completed Wordo sheets. This provides a quick reminder that the red word set goes with the red-dot Wordo cards. During a subsequent lesson, write a new word-card set in blue. The children write a new set of words on the reverse of the red-dot sheet and code it with a blue dot. Now the class has two sets of words and sheets that can easily be reused and reviewed.

drawing an index word card randomly and using it in a sentence.

2. The children cover that word on their Wordo sheets using scraps of paper, beans, or buttons.

The game continues until someone has filled in a horizontal, vertical, or diagonal line. That child calls out each word, spells it, and *cross-checks* with the word cards.

Variation:

◆ When children are comfortable with the Wordo game format, invite students to select their own set of words from the Word Wall. However, to avoid extending games too long, limit word selection through specific qualifications. For example, students may be asked to select only three letter words, words with multi-letter onsets, or those between *A* and *F* on the Word Wall. These qualifiers also provide informal, yet very informative, assessments of children's understanding of targeted concepts.

Activity—Scribble-Scrabble

Strategy used: cross-checking

This popular game borrows from the format of Scrabble™. Give each child a set of Word Tiles. In pairs or small groups, the children combine the sets and place them face down on the table (or floor). The game proceeds as follows:

1. Each child selects seven tiles.

2. By rolling a die, one child is chosen to go first and tries to make a word using as many of his or her seven tiles as possible. (If playing for points, each tile used is worth 1 point.)

3. The word is placed in the center of the table, and the child replaces any used tiles from the remaining overturned tiles.

4. The next child then tries to make a new word, extending from—or using a letter within—the existing word, much like the game Scrabble.

5. If that child is unsuccessful, the turn passes to the next player.

6. When the children are uncertain about the appropriateness of a peer's word, they can *cross-check* using the Word Wall or a dictionary.

Activity—Word Searches and Puzzles

Strategy used: thinking aloud

Word searches and puzzles are great for reviewing Word Wall or Theme-Builder words.

✱ Use grid paper to create Word Searches. Students write in the selected words, and then fill in any remaining spaces with random letters. (A Word Search

▲ Word Search is one of many instructional games that reinforce word-level strategies.

template is included at the end of the chapter.) They can swap the completed sheets with a neighbor, copy them into a special book to take home, or you can laminate them to use in a Learning Center.

✳ Create *crossword puzzles* with the children, modeling the process for them. They'll need plenty of practice with the format. Place selected words onto a grid and have the class make suggestions for the puzzle clues. Model how you *think aloud* to create appropriate definitions. As they gain experience, children can work in pairs or teams to develop their own puzzles to stump their peers (or their parents)!

In this chapter we've explored a variety of issues related to word study, including the often controversial topics of phonics and vocabulary. Word- and letter-level strategies are essential components of any strategies-based classroom. It's also critical to recognize that these concepts are most effective when introduced and practiced at the point of use. Not all young children will be ready for the concepts at the same time, nor will all children benefit from the same toolbox of strategies. It's important to:

◆ provide children with meaningful exposure to many strategies

◆ model strategy use as part of authentic literacy experiences

◆ focus on those words that are meaningful and developmentally appropriate for your group of students

◆ carefully observe children's reading and writing

Don't forget to step back and have fun with the craft of learning words!

Letter Home

WHAT ABOUT PHONICS?

Dear Parents and Caregivers,

The ability to figure out words and letter sounds is an important concept for any child learning to read. After all, the English alphabet is made up of symbols, or letters, that represent a particular set of sounds. What might look different, however, is the way we teach letters and sounds as part of strategies-based literacy instruction.

Will phonics really be taught? The answer to that is simple—Absolutely! Phonics is no less important to a strategies-centered teacher than any other instructional approach. What will be different, however, are the types of activities your child will engage in. For example, many teachers have found that worksheets are simply not as effective as other types of activities. Isolating sounds and practicing them through paper and pencil drills doesn't necessarily help children learn to read and write. Similarly, memorizing rules is often ineffective.

So how is phonics taught? Instead of isolating sounds or memorizing rules, we actively involve children in strategies-centered classrooms in discovering word patterns by using Word Tiles, reading and being read to daily, sorting words and sounds, and focusing on those words that they encounter most frequently. Most important, children are learning to use their strategies independently to figure out new words in print.

What about vocabulary instruction? Like phonics, vocabulary instruction also plays a very important role in a strategies-centered classroom. Your child will be focusing on sight words—those words that we all encounter most frequently when we read—through activities incorporating Word Walls and Word Tiles. Children who become familiar with the most common words in our language blossom as independent readers!

Word Wall

Aa		Bb		Cc
a	and	back	big	came
about	are	bank	boy	can
all	as	be	bug	car
am	at	because	but	children
an		best	by	come
				could

Dd	Ee	Ff	Gg	
day	each	find	get	good
did	eat	for	girl	got
do		friend	give	
don't		from	go	
down		fun	going	

Hh		Ii	Jj	Kk
had	here	I	jump	kick
has	him	if	just	know
have	his	in		
he	home	is		
her	how	it		

Ll		Mm	Nn	
let	lot	made	name	now
like		make	new	
line		me	night	
little		more	no	
look		my	not	

Word Wall

Oo		Pp	Qq	Rr
of	other	play	question	rain
off	out			ride
old	over			
one				
or				

Ss		Tt		
said	so	talk	them	this
saw	some	tell	then	time
school	stop	that	there	to
see		the	they	too
she		their	thing	trip
				two

Uu	Vv	Ww		
up	very	want	what	will
us		was	when	with
use		we	where	would
		went	who	
		were	why	

Xx	Yy	Zz	How to use the Word Wall:
	yes	zoo	
	you		• Read the words together.
	your		• Make up sentences.
			• Find the words in stories.
			• Make up rhyming words.
			• Play Wordo or Concentration.
			• Guess the Mystery Word.
			• Hunt for the words on cereal boxes.
			• Write a new story.

Teaching Reading Strategies in the Primary Grades Scholastic Professional Books

Word Wall Checklist

Word Wall Word	Date Introduced	Date Reviewed

Name _____

Individual Word Wall Checklist

Word Wall Word	Date Introduced	Date Reviewed

Teaching Reading Strategies in the Primary Grades Scholastic Professional Books

W	O	R	D	O
		FREE SPACE		

Word **S**earch

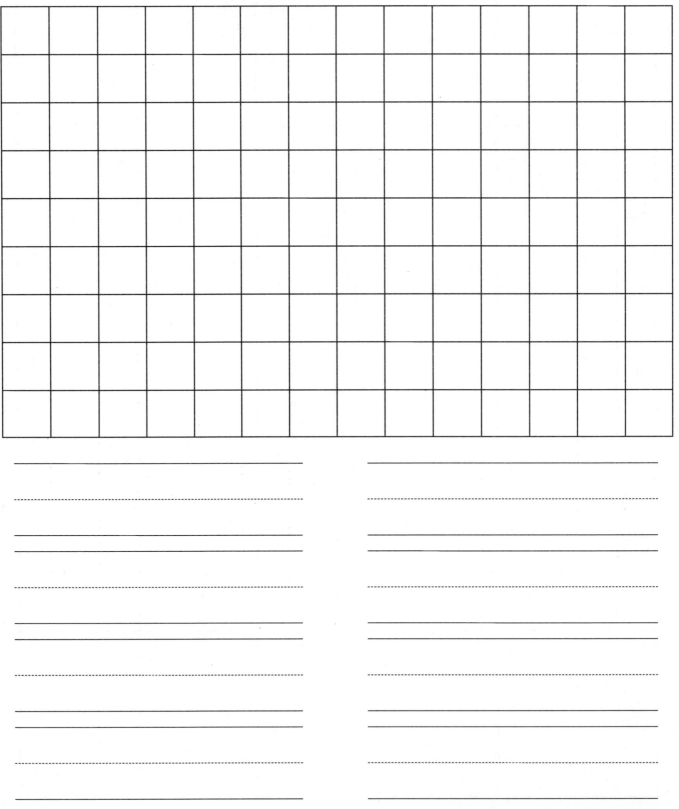

Teaching Reading Strategies in the Primary Grades Scholastic Professional Books

Chapter References

Cunningham, P. M. *Phonics They Use: Words for Reading and Writing*. New York: HarperCollins, 1995.

Cunningham, P. M., and Allington, R. L. *Classrooms that Work: They Can All Read and Write*. New York: Longman, 1999.

Cunningham, P. M., and Hall, D. P. Making Words: *Multilevel, Hands-On, Developmentally Appropriate Spelling and Phonics Activities*. Parsippany, NJ: Good Apple, 1994.

Dahl, K. L., and Scharer, P.L. "Phonics Teaching and Learning in Whole Language Classrooms: New Evidence from Research." *The Reading Teacher*, 53, no. 7 (April, 2000): 584-594.

Fields, M. V., and Spangler, K.L. *Let's Begin Reading Right: Developmentally Appropriate Beginning Literacy*. Columbus, OH: Prentice-Hall, 1995.

Juel, C. and Minden-Cupp, C. "Learning to Read Words: Linguistic Units and Instructional Strategies." *Reading Research Quarterly*. 35, no. 4 (October/November, December, 2000): 458-492.

Stahl, S.A. "Saying the 'P' Word: Nine Guidelines for Exemplary Phonics Instruction." *The Reading Teacher*. 45, no. 8 (April, 1992): 618-625.

Stahl, S.A., Duffy-Hester, A.M., and Stahl, K.A.D. "Everything You Wanted to Know About Phonics (But Were Afraid To Ask)." *Reading Research Quarterly*. 33, no. 3 (July/August/September, 1998): 338-355.

CHAPTER FOUR

Grouping—Strategy Circles, Learning Centers, and Book Clubs

Strategy Circles are critical to strategies-centered instruction

Strategy instruction can easily be integrated in a variety of informal ways across the literacy curriculum through explicit, direct instruction during whole-group reading activities (see Chapter 5) and in small groups.

* **Whole-group** activities allow time for the class to work collaboratively as a learning community around common texts and units.

* **Small groups** provide focused time on particular strategies using texts that are appropriate to a particular group of children.

In this chapter, we'll concentrate on small groups and provide insights into how to best configure and use small groups in a strategies-based classroom. In particular, we'll describe a specific technique that we've found most effective in introducing and modeling strategy use—the Strategy Circle. We'll explain how to set up Strategy Circles (which are small groups) and how they can be regularly scheduled as part of a broader-based Learning Center program. The role of Book Clubs in a strategies-centered classroom will also be discussed.

Strategy Circles

Strategy Circles are small, carefully selected, flexible groups of students who share common needs. Instruction focuses on specific strategies and texts that are appropriate for the children in these groups at a given point in time. It is scaffolded instruction that builds on what the children already know. And we've found that Strategy Circles avoid the difficulties often associated with ability grouping. (See "What the Experts Say" for more information.)

Strategy Circles incorporate many of the same activities as a guided-reading session, but the purposes are different. Typically, the purpose of guided reading is to focus on reading comprehension (see Chapter 5). The primary emphasis during Strategy Circles, however, is directly on strategy use—including the modeling, practice, and review of strategies that a specific group of students is ready to learn.

What the Experts Say About . . .

Grouping

What is wrong with typical ability groups? Typical ability groups are often rigid and static. They differentiate instruction and lock children—particularly those struggling with reading—into the same group status over long periods of time. This hinders growth because not all children develop at the same pace. Lower reading groups tend to focus more on skills and lower-level thinking at the expense of actual reading and comprehension. Thus traditional ability groups favor more proficient readers, widening the gap between the best and worst readers in a classroom.

What can make grouping more effective? Young children can be grouped according to skill, interest, work habits, knowledge of strategies, task, social considerations, random selection, and student choice. The key is variety and flexibility—to ensure that children will use their strengths and interact collaboratively.

What about Strategy Circles? In these carefully selected groups, teachers can tailor direct instruction to each child's specific needs and bridge his or her experiences to new concepts and knowledge. This scaffolding that occurs in Strategy Circles is essential in building children's independence. With Strategy Circles, children learn to read with materials at their level, and teachers can foster their potential as readers by continually moving them just beyond what they can do alone.

Sources: Campana, Pickenpaugh, Henry, and Wiley, 2000; Fawson and Reutzel, 2000; Flood, Lapp, Flood, and Nagel, 1992; Opitz, 1999; Schulman and Payne, 2000.

How to Form and Evaluate Strategy Circles

To avoid some of the common pitfalls of ability grouping and maintain successful Strategy Circles, you'll need to form and monitor your Circle groups carefully. It's important to change the groups' membership regularly to be sure that each child is always in a Circle with peers of similar strengths and abilities.

Effective Grouping . . .

◆ is flexible in terms of group membership and format (Strategy Circles, interests, content, concepts, and so on).

◆ provides ample opportunities for children to read.

◆ matches the task to the grouping format.

◆ matches children with books at their instructional level.

◆ relies on careful observation and ongoing, informal assessment.

◆ keeps group size small, particularly for readers who are struggling.

◆ provides useful observations of children's progress.

◆ is balanced with a variety of whole and small group activities.

Less Effective Grouping . . .

◆ keeps group membership static over time.

◆ uses the same text for all children during directed instruction.

◆ applies labels to groups and children.

◆ relies on a textbook or commercial materials for skill sequence, instead of children's needs.

◆ uses only one type of grouping exclusively (either whole or small groups).

Strategy Assessment

In addition to observing your young readers carefully to monitor students' growth in strategy learning, incorporate informal assessments into your literacy instruction. A variety of assessments are available. Two particularly useful assessments are Running Records and Strategy Interviews (described on page 93). Through such assessments, you can effectively form and reform your Strategy Circles.

▲ Informal assessments are invaluable in determining how individual students use strategies.

Tips for Success with Running Records

* Administer the Running Records individually, with as few distractions as possible.

* Start with an easy text and build to more difficult pieces.

* Use short, interesting pieces from different genres and across multiple grade levels.

* If possible, have more than one piece available for each level.

* In order to accurately record a student's errors (miscues), have children read from actual texts or exact copies of the book, not a retyped version, so he or she can use picture and text formatting clues.

* If you must retype the text, include the same phrasing and font style.

* When a child gets stuck on a word, avoid giving it too quickly. Allow enough time for the child to try out a variety of strategies independently.

* Continue with more difficult texts until the child s fluency and/or comprehension breaks down.

* When you're finished, offer congratulations for a terrific job!

☑ Running Records

Using a Running Record Evaluation Sheet (sample on page 95; reproducible at end of the chapter), sit with an individual child to record and follow his or her reading progress in detail. Running Records will help you determine each child's reading level and use of strategies. Many commercial Running Record protocols are available, and some reading basals incorporate Running Records into their assessment

Acquiring sets of texts for Strategy Circles can take creative planning. You might explore using district grants or funds set aside for classroom consumables. Also don't overlook the possibility of sharing titles with other teachers at your grade level.

However, if you don't have access to a set of leveled texts, use short, but complete, passages from a reading basal or an anthology. Because it's important to use texts that children are *not* familiar with, an unused series is best. If possible, cut stories out of the bound basal so you can easily organize and file them.

plans. You can easily adapt these resources for your own use or develop a modified version (see *Taking Running Records* by Mary Shea, Scholastic, 2000). Here are some guidelines:

1. **Select a set of short books of increasing difficulty.** Many publishers now provide such "leveled" sets, or guides, for determining the approximate level of a variety of books.

2. **Start with a text that you believe the child you are assessing can read fluently.** Observe him or her read the book out loud, noting the number and type of errors, or miscues. Observe the child's fluency and use of strategies carefully.

3. **Ask brief, probing questions at the end of each piece to check on story comprehension.** This step is important because some children can read very fluently but don't really understand what they read (and vice versa).

4. **Have the child continue to read increasingly difficult texts until he or she reaches a point of frustration (frustrational level).** You'll know when you've reached that point because the child can't read fluently and makes enough errors to affect comprehension of the story.

5. **Then consider the book the child read before the point of frustration as that child's approximate "instructional" reading level.** A text that is at a child's instructional level is one that's challenging enough to require him or her to use strategies to decode the text and acquire meaning, but not so difficult that comprehension is inaccessible.

☑ Recorded Records

Another assessment involves tape recording each child reading the same grade-level text passage at the beginning, middle, and end of the year. These recordings provide concrete documentation of a child's growth in fluency and use of strategies over time. And most children love to hear themselves on tape!

Administer Running Records monthly so you can make appropriate adjustments in your Strategy Circle groupings and systematically monitor children's progress. We usually take Running Records during individual conferences that are part of the children's self-selected reading (see Chapter 5).

Running Records

Running Records are an informative tool for determining a child's approximate reading level and use of strategies. The *Running Record Evaluation Sheet* form is located at the end of this chapter.

This tool examines:

Error Rate. You can use this simple equation to determine the rate of errors a child makes. Determining the child's instructional level (text that's not too easy or too hard) is the focus of Running Records.

Fluency. Examine the child's reading fluency with the criteria listed. They often indicate the text comprehension and the automaticity with which he or she integrates strategies.

Word Analysis. Write miscues in the first column of the chart and the word the child read instead in the next. If the child realized the error and reread the miscued word correctly check the "self-correction" column. If the child skipped a word, check the "omitted" column.

Strategies Observed. Check strategies the child used independently. These records are invaluable for planning future instruction.

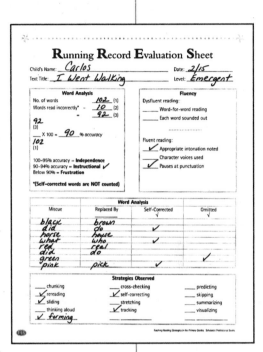

☑ Strategy Interviews

Like Running Records, Strategy Interviews provide information about a child's knowledge of strategy use. Unlike Running Records, however, children do not read a text. Instead they discuss how they perceive their own strategy use. These interviews also provide you with the opportunity to find out how much a child understands about applying strategies to a variety of reading tasks.

The Strategy Interview that we've developed is based on four language cueing systems: pragmatics, grapho-phonemics, syntax, and semantics. (See reproducible Interview at end of chapter.)

◆ **Pragmatics** describes the context of the reading activity and how different tasks affect how we read. For example, most of us would approach the task of reading a physics text quite differently from browsing through newspaper ads.

◆ **Grapho-phonemics** refers to the sound-symbol relationships in our language. Specifically, this part of the interview focuses on children's perceptions of word-level strategies.

- **Syntax** refers to the grammatical structure of our language and often involves the analysis of sentence construction.

- **Semantics** involves the construction of meaning while reading and therefore taps a child's use of text-level strategies.

We found that by using these cueing systems as the basis of our interview young children could perceive that there were differences among the strategies they would select to figure out unknown words (grapho-phonemics) and to make meaning of the text (semantics).

Strategy Interview Hints

- ✳ Administer the Strategy Interview in a one-on-one setting during Morning Work or self-selected reading conferences.

- ✳ Strategy Interviews should occur only twice a year. They serve as a less formal indicator of students' use and understanding of classroom strategies than Running Records.

- ✳ Because it is important that children have some knowledge of strategies to be successful with the Interview, introduce it mid-way through the year and then again during the final weeks of school.

Administering the Interview

The actual administration of the Strategy Interview requires very little advance preparation.

1. **Select a few samples of texts commonly used in the classroom.** We've used a familiar picture book, a ring of Word Wall words (a set of index cards bound with a metal ring), and poem charts. For older children, consider selecting a variety of genres to use as a comparison.

2. **Begin the interview by asking the child to look at the selected items and discuss how reading one item, such as the ring of words, would differ from reading the book.** More sophisticated readers will approach the task of reading a list of isolated words quite differently than reading a complete text.

3. **For the following sections of the interview, give the child the book to use as a reference to answer questions.** Ask how he or she would decipher an unknown word (grapho-phonemics), make sense from a difficult sentence (syntax), and construct meaning from a passage (semantics). For each question, prompt the child to use the book to demonstrate using strategies.

4. **End the interview by asking the child if there are any questions for the teacher.** This twist puts the session's very one-sided interaction back into the hands of the child.

5. Using the Results. One of the most valuable uses of the Strategy Interview is in finding gaps in instruction or strategies that might need particular emphasis. These findings help guide the development of subsequent Strategy Circle instruction.

Preparing and Conducting Strategy Circles

Running Records and Strategy Interviews provide invaluable information for selecting group members for Strategy Circles. Before implementing the Circles, you'll also need to prepare some specific instructional materials.

☑ **Getting Ready**

1. **Choose multiple copies of books in a range of reading levels.**

2. *Prepare a large strategy chart to provide the focus for instruction.* These charts will differ across grade levels and will reflect the needs of individual classes of children. First, select those strategies best suited for your students; then create visual cues for each strategy. For example, we use a picture of a giraffe's long neck as a cue for *stretching*. Post the cues with the strategies on a large classroom chart, which is used as a consistent reference for whole-group activities.

3. **Create smaller versions of the chart to use during Strategy Circles time.** Reducing the chart onto 8.5- by 11-inch paper works well.

4. **Create strategy cards by cutting extra laminated copies of the strategy chart into separate index-sized cards.** Store the card sets in plastic zipper bags.

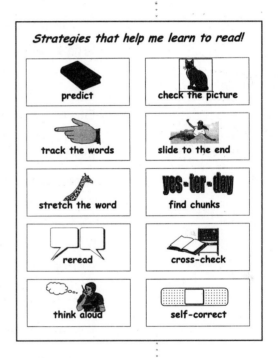

Strategies that help me learn to read!

predict · check the picture · track the words · slide to the end · stretch the word · find chunks · reread · cross-check · think aloud · self-correct

☑ **Introducing the Strategies**

It's important to familiarize both the children and their caregivers with the strategies:

◆ During whole-group or Word Wall lessons, refer to the large strategy chart to explain and model the strategies you're using.

◆ Use the chart as a reference when you read aloud or write a group story.

◆ During Back to School night, review the strategies with the children's caregivers by pointing them out on the chart.

◆ Provide a copy of the chart for each caregiver to take home. This way, the family can reinforce what their children are learning in the classroom. (See "Send-Home Ideas.")

- Include reminders of selected strategies in send-home notes.

- Revisit the strategy chart during parent conferences. By then, you can share where each child is developmentally and which strategies are most useful for that child.

■ ■ ■ ■ ■ ■ ■ ■ ■ ■ ■ ■ ■ ■ ■

Strategy Sessions

There are many ways to involve families with their children's strategy lessons. Home review and reinforcement help make strategy use more automatic for children and give them practice in applying their strategies across different settings. Specific ideas for home involvement include:

* **Send a copy of the class Strategy Chart home with each child.** Invite the children to explain the strategies to their parents/caregivers and encourage family members to use the chart as a reference when they read with the child.

* **Encourage family members to talk about the strategies that they use when they read and write.** Have the children report back to the class, and then add new strategies the class Chart when appropriate.

* **Over a one or two day period, invite the children to keep a tally of the strategies they use when they read aloud to their caregivers.** Combine all the children's responses in a class tally.

* **Have parents/caregivers and their children work together on making strategy bookmarks to use at home.** Suggest they include new visual cues on the bookmarks.

* **Select a new strategy to try each night for a week.** Have the children share those they found the most useful with their Strategy Circle.

* **Ask children to tape record themselves reading a favorite story at home** (without adult interruption). Then have the children and their caregivers listen to the tape and jot down the strategies used.

☑ Organizing Materials for Strategy Circles

To smooth transitions for Strategy Circle time, prepare Strategy Baskets with materials for each group. This organization helps in those situations where you can have an adult volunteer take over one of the Strategy Circles. Basket materials include:

- Multiple copies of a book at that group's instructional level.

- A pocket folder, with copies of lesson plans for that title from the teacher's manual (when available).

- Sight and/or Word Wall words that correspond to the text written on index cards.
- Laminated graphic organizers.
- Letter-sized copy of the classroom strategy chart.
- Individual cue cards for each of the strategies.
- Strategy-Circle Observation Forms.

☑ Scheduling Strategy Circles

There are many ways to schedule Strategy Circles into a strategies-based literacy classroom. It's important to be flexible and to provide plenty of time for children to read texts at their instructional levels so they can practice the strategies they need most.

Strategy Circles can be part of:

- ❋ Morning Work
- ❋ Independent reading or writing
- ❋ Learning Centers (page 106)
- ❋ Shoebox activities (Chapter 5).

Or they may be planned periodically in place of:

- ❋ Whole-group directed instruction
- ❋ Spelling or phonics lessons

☑ Conducting Strategy-Circle Sessions

There is no one prescription for using Strategy Circles. However, the following is a good format for early lessons, which will typically last about 10 minutes.

1. **Review the Strategies.** Begin with a quick review of each of the strategies on the chart and ask the children what strategies they use when they get stuck on a word or on the meaning of a story.

2. **Reinforce the Strategies.** As the children suggest strategies, show the individual strategy cue cards for further reinforcement. Also match the cue cards with the large, class chart and remind students to use this chart as a reference if they are having difficulty with reading and writing.

3. **Introduce the Story.** As each Strategy Circle group reads from texts that are at an appropriate instructional level . . .

   - Have the students look at the book's title and cover illustration to *predict* what it will be about.

   - Invite the group to take a picture walk through the book, *checking* the illustrations to make further predictions about the content.

- Review any potentially unfamiliar vocabulary essential to the story's meaning.

- Model the strategy of *cross-checking* as you match sight words in the text to words on the Word Wall or on other classroom displays.

4. **Read the Text.** Have the children read the story aloud chorally or silently to themselves.

- Then, have them take turns *rereading* portions of the story. Here's a chance for you to hear how individual children are applying strategies.

- In other Circle sessions, ask students to read independently or with a partner; a variety of formats provides practice with different contexts.

5. **Focus on One Strategy.** After completing the story, ask the children which strategies they used while reading the day's text. They can refer to the small chart or cue cards. Then, select one strategy to focus on with the group. Choose a strategy that is useful for reading that day's text, or one that reinforces a lesson using a strategy you've recently introduced.

6. **Recap.** As time permits, introduce comprehension activities. For example, you might have the children discuss their favorite character in the story, share new facts they learned, or compare this story with a similar one they have read before.

- As a reinforcement of the day's instruction, send the book home for children to reread with a family member.

Sample Lesson

Strategy Circle

A small group has gathered on the floor of the reading corner, circled around Melody. She puts the group strategy chart to the side, but in view of the children.

"Today, we're going to start a new story," Melody begins. "This story tells about some animals in the ocean. We've been studying the ocean in class, but maybe we'll learn something new today. First, though, let's review some of the strategies we can use when we run into trouble while reading. Can anyone think of a strategy?"

"Slide to the end!" SueLynn responds. "That's what I like to do."

"That's an excellent strategy." Melody takes out the *slide to the end* card and places it in the center of the circle. "Anyone else?"

"I check for picture clues," Juel responds. "And sometimes I stretch out long words."

"Those are excellent strategies, too." Melody takes the *checking* and *stretching* cards out, and places them with the *sliding* card.

"Today, when we're reading our new story, I'd like you to think about a new strategy, *rereading*. Does anyone know what that is?" Melody holds up the *rereading* card.

"I do!" exclaims Miguel. "That's when you read something again. Like when you get stuck or something."

"That's exactly right, Miguel. When you're reading and something doesn't sound just right, sometimes it helps to reread, or read it again. I'll keep the *rereading* card close to me here to remind us of this new strategy when we read. Now, let's predict what this story is about. What does the cover tell us about the story?" Melody adds the *prediction* card to the others.

The group discusses the cover title and illustrations and makes predictions about the story. These predictions are *confirmed* as the group walks through the book and discusses the text's illustrations. When they're comfortable with the text, the group takes turns reading the story out loud and checking their initial predictions.

"Excellent reading! I noticed a couple things in this story. Did you see any Word Wall words that we've been studying in class?"

"I did! I saw *in, the, at,* and *then.*"

"Very good, Juel. I bet you used the strategy of *cross-checking* for those Word Wall words. I also heard you reread a tricky sentence on page five. Excellent use of that strategy." Melody places the *rereading* card with the others in the center of the circle. "Now, let's think of new facts that we learned in this book."

Miguel exclaims, "I learned that whales aren't fish!"

"Good job. Let's write that new fact in our Learning Logs. First, though, don't forget to write down the book title and date! Who can think of another new fact?"

☑ Strategy Circle Observations

One of the primary purposes of Strategy Circles is to provide specific information about which strategies the children are using independently and to gain ideas for incorporating strategies into subsequent lessons. One tool you can use to gather this information is a "Strategy Circle Observation Form" (see reproducible at the end of chapter). The observation form helps you keep track of what strategies are being used successfully and automatically, and which need to be introduced or reinforced. For example, when you observe a student *tracking* the text spontaneously as he or she reads aloud, place an *S* (for "Student observed using strategy") next to *tracking the words* on the form and jot down the child's name. Note the introduction of a strategy, *rereading* for example, with an *I*. An *M* indicates that you've *modeled* a particular

Strategy Circle Observation Form

Date: *March 5*

Students:
Juel
Joesifina
Stacey
mike

Description of activities:
- *Review strategies with strategy cards*
- *Preview "I Went Walking" using a picture walk*
- *choral read*
- *model how to self-correct*
- *List word wall words in Learning Logs*

Observations:
Joesifina didn't participate today—need to follow-up.
Juel may be ready for a new group. Plan Running Records for Tuesday.

Strategies Observed:
M predicting
M checking the picture
S tracking the words *Juel, Stacey, mike*
___ sliding to the end
___ stretching the word
S finding chunks *Juel ("at" in cat)*
P rereading - *focus on having the text "make sense"*
M cross-checking
___ thinking aloud
I self-correcting
_____

I= strategy introduced   R= strategy reviewed
M= teacher modeling of new strategy   P= plan for future session

strategy, and an *R* tells which strategies have been reviewed. By keeping track of the strategies introduced and reviewed, you can quickly identify which ones you've overlooked and then plan to include them in future lessons.

✳ Strategy Circle Activities

In addition to using the general format described, you can incorporate a variety of activities into Strategy Circle time to reinforce specific strategies.

Activity—Question Markers

Strategy used: questioning

Rich, interactive discussions are an important component of any Strategy Circle session. And one of the most difficult tasks in leading an effective book discussion is choosing appropriate and varied questions that focus and challenge readers at all levels. One very useful tool for ensuring quality in questioning is the "Question Marker." (See reproducible at the end of chapter.) Questions on one side of the marker focus on word-level strategies; text-level questions are on the flip side. After reading a book during Strategy Circle, use the marker to help guide discussion while you focus on specific strategies. It is important to select questions thoughtfully. Presenting the entire question inventory during a single discussion session, for instance, would overwhelm students!

Variations:

◆ Have the children use the markers to guide student-directed discussions.

◆ Put markers in Take Home folders for caregivers to use as they share texts with their children at home.

◆ Adapt the markers for various types of text. Include fiction and nonfiction.

Activity—Learning Logs

Strategies used: accessing, analyzing, cross-checking, focusing, summarizing, synthesizing

Learning Logs are a great accompaniment to Strategy Circles and Learning Centers (described later in this chapter). Inexpensive notebooks can serve as Logs or you can quickly create your own by stapling together blank sheets of paper. You (or your students) record the title of the book and the date, and then students complete activities like the following, which are easily adapted to the developmental levels of your students:

✳ List the strategies you used when you read today. Circle the strategy that worked the best.

✳ *Cross-check* using the Word Wall. How many Word Wall words can you find in this book?

* Write down any *rhyming* pairs you found in this book. Can you think of other words that rhyme with them? Write those new words in a different color.

* *Focus* by drawing a picture of an important event that happened in the story. If you were a character in the story, what might you have done differently?

* *Access* what you know about yourself by drawing a picture of your favorite character. How are you different from that character? How are you similar?

▲ A variety of graphic organizers can be included in Learning Logs.

* Draw a picture of how you feel after reading the text. Describe your feelings in a short story or poem.

* *Synthesize* what you read. Write down two questions about the book. Pass your log to your neighbor and see if he or she can answer your questions.

* *Focus* on the most important facts in the book and write down all the new things you learned. What else would you like to know?

* *Synthesize* the story by writing about another book that this one reminds you of. What is the same? What is different?

* *Summarize* the story by writing a book critique.

Activity—Graphic Organizers

Strategies used: accessing, analyzing, focusing, monitoring, questioning, summarizing

Graphic organizers are a great way to review text-level strategies. (Reproducibles for each of the examples are included at end of chapter.) Before they read, students paste the graphic organizer sheet into their logs.

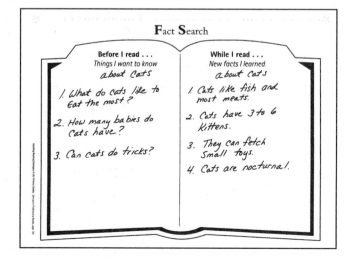

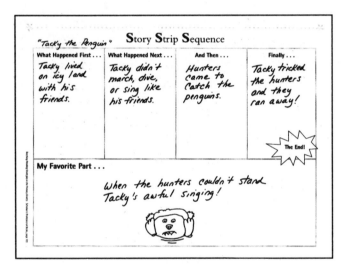

Character Comparison

Character #1	How They Are The Same	Character #2
Clifford		*Emily Elizabeth*
is a dog big has fur hides catches cars does tricks chews shoes	have fun together like to play games live in a house	is a girl small has hair finds

"Tacky the Penguin" **Story Strip Sequence**

What Happened First . . .	What Happened Next . . .	And Then . . .	Finally . . .
Tacky lived on icy land with his friends.	Tacky didn't march, dive, or sing like his friends.	Hunters came to catch the penguins.	Tacky tricked the hunters and they ran away!

The End!

My Favorite Part . . .

When the hunters couldn't stand Tacky's awful singing!

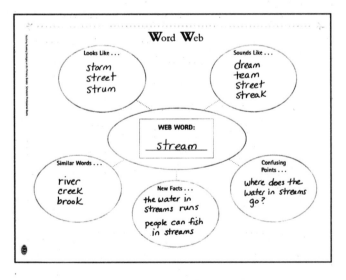

Word Web

Looks Like . . .
storm
street
strum

Sounds Like . . .
dream
team
street
streak

WEB WORD:
stream

Similar Words . . .
river
creek
brook

New Facts . . .
the water in streams runs

people can fish in streams

Confusing Points . . .
where does the water in streams go?

◆ **Fact Search.** They use the fact sheet form to write what they want to learn from the text and the new facts they discover *while* reading. This activity helps the children fine-tune the *focusing* strategy. Because they use it is as they read, it also enhances the *monitoring* strategy.

◆ **Character Comparison.** Students *analyze* the text by either comparing two characters in a story or by comparing themselves with one of the characters.

◆ **Story Sequence.** This chart, which is formatted like a simple comic strip, enhances the strategy of *summarizing*. Students either write or draw events in the sequence of the story and write a description of their favorite part. Cut out the sequence part of the form and combine it with other student's sequences to make a group Comic Book.

◆ **Word Web.** Write an unfamiliar or key concept in the center of this graphic organizer. Children use the cues provided (*looks like, similar words, new facts, and so on*) to access what they already know about the word and to provide the focus for questioning while *rereading* the text.

You can use lots of other formats to emphasize strategies in *summarizing* and *analyzing* the text. Those shown here can be adapted to a variety of texts and Learning Log experiences.

Activity—Bookmarks

Strategies used: individualized to the child

Individualize strategy sessions by creating personal bookmarks that include four to five strategies that are most useful for each child. Keep the bookmarks in the book tubs that children use during self-selected reading

(Chapter 5). Bookmarks provide a quick reference to those strategies that help them the most as they read independently.

☑ Strategy Circle Performances

Even the shiest children become less inhibited when they transform themselves into the role of a favorite character. And performances are another way to informally assess students' understanding of a story. Children's interpretations reveal a great deal about their understanding of story sequence and character traits.

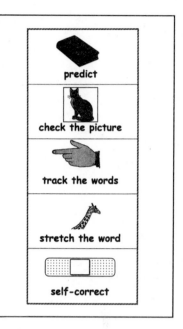

predict

check the picture

track the words

stretch the word

self-correct

▲ Creative performances reinforce text comprehension.

❋ Performance Activities

Activity—Readers' Theater

Strategies used: analyzing, focusing, summarizing

One of the easiest forms of performance is Readers' Theater (the simple reenactment of a story using books) because it doesn't require props or memorization. Readers' Theater is particularly appropriate for Strategy Circles, as time is often quite limited. Readers' Theater naturally reinforces the strategies of *analyzing* and *summarizing*, and can be performed in a variety of formats, including the following:

❋ Children read from scripts that they've written as their Strategy Circles jointly *summarize* the story's events.

✳ One child (the narrator) guides the story summary, and the others assume the roles of the characters. Rather than reading from the book verbatim, children follow along in their books as they describe their character's actions and story's events. This provides a quick assessment of their ability to *focus* on important elements in the story.

Activity—Puppets

Strategy used: summarizing

Simple puppets also fit into the timeframe of Strategy Circles. Children can quickly make puppets using paper bags, socks, gloves, construction paper, and Popsicle sticks or straws. Have the children assume the role of one of the book's characters and *summarize* the story or read the dialogue directly from the text. Reading gives practice in recognizing quotation marks in print; summarizing provides an *authentic* review. Students can share their Strategy Circle performances with the rest of the class, or videotape them to be enjoyed at an Open House or other special classroom event.

Activity—Nonfiction Performances

Strategies used: accessing, focusing, questioning

Adapt nonfiction books for a group performance. For example, after reading a book on oceans, have each child assume the role of one of the aquatic animals they studied. First, have them access their own knowledge about the animal as they *question* themselves to *check* their understanding. The children *focus* on important information as they read the book and write down facts about their animal. Then they can share their reports with peers, taking turns reading them aloud.

Variations:

◆ Combine puppets with the presentation.

◆ Children can assume the role of famous characters in history books and focus on the facts by being interviewed by a "reporter."

Learning Centers and Strategy Circles

Explicit strategy instruction is most effective when it's presented to small groups of children with similar needs. In addition, providing a variety of small-group Learning Center activities is effective in reinforcing learning and fostering young children's skills in collaboration and communication. Therefore, we've found that incorporating teacher- (or aide-/volunteer-) led Strategy Circles into a classroom

Learning Centers

Incorporating Learning Centers into the primary classroom provides many academic benefits.

Carefully planned Learning Centers with specific learning objectives . . .

✳ foster an atmosphere that is based on constructivism and child-centered learning.

✳ increase responsibility, ownership of learning, and confidence.

✳ promote students' decision-making skills.

✳ encourage self-evaluation.

✳ promote communication and collaboration as children solve problems together.

Creating effective Centers requires advance planning and a focus on instructional goals. It's important to:

✳ take the time to introduce each activity and establish clear routines.

✳ design Center activities around district/state curriculum guidelines.

✳ develop Centers with clear objectives that are fully integrated into the curriculum.

✳ involve children directly in creating the Centers by having them share items related to the topic, suggest books or activities, or write directions for their classmates.

Sources: Burpo and Wheeler, 1994; Novelli, 1995; Patton and Mercer, 1996; Snowden and Christian, 1998.

Learning Center format works well. The children in such Strategy Circle groups are the same as those in the Learning Center groups. (Depending on the type of activity, groups are sometimes split or joined.) This system maximizes students' time on task, ensures that strategy sessions are scheduled regularly (at least once a week), and enhances the potential that students' strategy use will carry over to Center activities.

Learning Centers laced with Strategy Circles provide young children with the chance to explore a variety of hands-on activities while they practice using strategies and to gain skills in independence and responsibility. (See "What the Experts Say About . . . .")

Centers in Action

Looking inside Melody's classroom during Learning Center time, you're likely to find one group of children listening intently to a story on tape to determine its sequence, which they'll later record in their Learning Logs. Four or so other children are at the classroom computer exploring a new program that takes them on an interactive adventure related to their class unit on expeditions. Another group, guided by a weekly parent volunteer, sits at a table working on math block patterns. Melody is on the floor in the reading corner with a Strategy Circle group reviewing the class Strategy Chart before starting a new book. The magic of this strategies-centered classroom is in the productive, purposeful engagement of each group of students with activities that are selected based on their needs and abilities.

Planning for Learning Centers

◆ **Begin Learning Centers a few months into the school year.** You'll be allowing time for your students to learn the routines of the classroom and for you to collect information about their approximate reading levels. You'll also have time to introduce strategies to the whole class, providing a scaffold for later, more focused sessions.

◆ **When you first introduce Learning Centers keep them short.** Fifteen minutes is sufficient. Later in the year, as concepts and lessons become more sophisticated, allot more time.

◆ **Spread Centers around the room to maximize space.** Some Learning Centers require more space than others, and some can be impromptu, created right at students' tables.

◆ **Limit the number of students at each Center.** We've found that having only three to five children at each Center is best.

How you schedule Learning Centers will reflect your own instructional routines. For example, Melody has found that scheduling Centers three times a week, for a two-week rotation, works best for her. Each group of students visits each of her six Centers over a two-week period. Melody creates a large chart of the group Center schedule, which she reviews with the children at the start of each rotation. At the end of the two weeks, Melody reassesses her groupings, makes adjustments as needed, and begins a new cycle.

Learning Center Rotation Schedule

	Day 1 (Week 1)	**Day 2** (Week 1)	**Day 3** (Week 1)	**Day 4** (Week 2)	**Day 5** (Week 2)	**Day 6** (Week 3)
Strategy Circle (Teacher)	Red Group	Orange Group	Yellow Group	Green Group	Blue Group	Purple Group
Volunteer Center (Parent)	Orange Group	Yellow Group	Green Group	Blue Group	Purple Group	Red Group
Strategy Circle (Aide)	Yellow Group	Green Group	Blue Group	Purple Group	Red Group	Orange Group
Listening Center	Green Group	Blue Group	Purple Group	Red Group	Orange Group	Yellow Group
Computer Center	Blue Group	Purple Group	Red Group	Orange Group	Yellow Group	Green Group
Literacy Center (Parent)	Purple Group	Red Group	Orange Group	Yellow Group	Green Group	Blue Group

✳ Learning Center Activities

Learning Center formats and topics will vary according to your instructional needs and the interests of your students. Strategy Circle centers are teacher- or aide-led, and specific strategy use is modeled and practiced. Some of the other Centers we've used include:

✳ *Curriculum-Based Centers.* These feature hands-on activities that relate to the content or literacy unit under study by the class. For example, as part of a unit on nutrition, students might create pattern beads with colored noodles, "purchase" grocery items, measure objects, and create graphs.

✳ *Listening Center.* In this self-directed Center, students listen to a story on tape and then respond to the text in their Learning Logs. Sometimes the taped book is an old favorite; other times it corresponds to a class unit or author study.

✳ *Computer Center.* Many teachers have student computer stations in their classrooms, but it can be difficult to schedule time for students to use them. Our Center system enables us to build-in regular computer use for all students. Be sure to provide a variety of programs for students to explore, including digitalized books, drawing programs, and language concept practice.

✳ *Literacy Center.* This Center provides hands-on activities in areas related to literacy instruction. For example, students might create a group poster for a book you've just read, perform a short Readers' Theater, write riddles to share with the class, or practice Word Wall words by playing Wordo.

Most of the non-Strategy Circle centers can be planned so that children can work independently—and gain confidence in using strategies on their own.

Keep Learning Centers Flexible

Regardless of which activities you use, Centers must remain flexible. For example, minimizing the number of groups would be more feasible for some classrooms. In others, a five-day rotation schedule would best suit the instructional needs of the class. There will also be those unexpected days when the parent volunteers you're counting on are not available or when technology breaks down. To counter these potential glitches, here are a few hints:

1. *Make sure that students clearly understand what is expected of them while working in the Centers.* Establish routines that clearly define these expectations and review them before each Center rotation.

2. *Have back-up ideas prepared in case of unforeseen interruptions.* For example, incorporate self-selected reading or student-created Word Games (see Chapter 3) as Center activities. One of Melody's students brought in a sophisticated space game related to the class's current unit, which he supervised in an impromptu

Center. Children also enjoy playing school, and you can direct them to lead Word Wall review activities.

3. *Schedule adequate time for less proficient readers to focus on strategy use.* For some young readers, even a daily short Strategy Circle meeting is simply not enough, despite the many whole-group lessons throughout each day. Get help! Tap the talents of a Title I aide, the pre-service and student teachers from a local university, or even college professors!

4. *If you find that two Strategy Circle groups have similar needs, combine the groups.* This doubles their total instructional time.

Again, the bottom line is flexibility—not only in grouping the children, but also in designing instructional time that adjusts to their needs.

Book Clubs—An Alternative Grouping

Book Clubs have become very popular with adults, and even television celebrities, as a way to dialogue with interested peers about books, common interests, and literacy. Similarly, young children can join Classroom Book Clubs to share favorite stories and authors. Book Clubs build on the natural connections between meaningful discussions and the social aspects of learning. Children's Book Club

▲ Classroom Book Clubs engage children in meaningful conversations with classmates.

conversations can be powerful and sustaining. Classroom Book Clubs can also provide the forum for discussing children's increasing knowledge of reading strategies.

Organizing Book Clubs

You can organize Book Clubs in a variety of ways, depending in part the texts selected and the purposes for the sessions. Clubs might tap students' interests in various hobbies or sports. For example, one group might focus on books about rock collecting, while another compares books on pet care. Often, however, you'll want the Clubs to support unit- or author-study. These Clubs extend classroom instruction and give students the chance to further explore aspects of the unit with classmates who share similar interests.

You can integrate Book Clubs into the classroom literacy routines in a variety of ways. Book Clubs can . . .

◆ replace Learning Centers once each month.

◆ be added into regular Center rotations.

◆ be an alternative to Morning Work.

◆ periodically replace whole-group guided reading.

◆ be offered during after-school activities.

Book Club Sessions

Children can engage in a variety of activities as part of their Book Club sessions—ranging from simple conversations—reading together and then talking about the book—to extended projects. (See "Expansions" that follow.) Some specific ideas include:

✳ reading the text independently and writing about it in a letter to fellow Club members. (The letters serve as a springboard for Club-meeting discussions.)

✳ creating a group poster about the story.

✳ making character comparisons, sequencing the story, or telling about a favorite part. (See story-strip reproducible at end of chapter.)

✳ investigating unfamiliar terms to create a specialized group dictionary.

✳ rewriting the story's ending.

✳ making ads or critiques of the book.

✳ charting new facts.

✳ sharing favorite parts of the book.

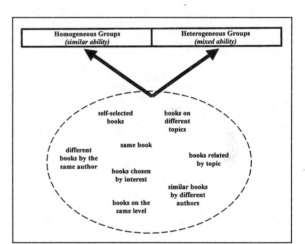

Homogeneous Groups (similar ability)	Heterogeneous Groups (mixed ability)

self-selected books

books on different topics

same book

different books by the same author

books related by topic

books chosen by interest

similar books by different authors

books on the same level

✳ comparing different books with similar themes.

For example, after reading *Five Little Monkeys Jumping on the Bed* by Eileen Christelow (Houghton Mifflin, 1998) and *Five Ugly Monsters* by Tedd Arnold (Scholastic, 1995), have the children complete a Venn diagram comparing events and characters in the two stories.

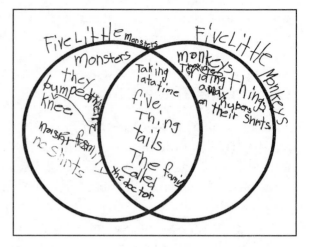

Expansions ◆◆◆◆◆◆◆◆◆◆◆◆◆◆◆◆◆◆

Book Clubs

Book Clubs can be extended to focus on children's higher-order thinking, with a particular emphasis on text-level strategies.

Activities that support *analyzing*:

◆ Each Club member selects one character to *analyze* by writing (or drawing) as many descriptors as possible. The child then shares the description with his or her peers, who try to guess the character.

◆ Club members *analyze* the characters through a self-comparison. How are they and the characters alike? Different? What actions in the story might each child do differently and why?

◆ The children compare and *analyze* story events. For example, each child selects one event in the story that he or she feels is the most important and explains why.

◆ The Club compares fiction and nonfiction texts. The children select an event in the story and use local newspaper articles to compare it to a similar one that has occurred in the community. They then *analyze* differences in outcomes.

Activities that support *summarizing*

◆ Club members visually summarize a text, either fiction or nonfiction, by creating a geographical map tracing events that occurred in the book.

◆ Children write story summaries as book critiques. Before reading their book, they read published critiques and list elements of effective persuasion. After reading the book, they use these elements to create their own literary critiques.

Activities that support *visualizing*

◆ After reading a book, children each select a scene that is described in the text, *visualize* it, and draw a picture of it. The children share their creations with other Club Members, who try to match the scene with the event in the book.

◆ One child reads a section of a new book to the other Club members, who focus on *visualizing* the scene or event. Each member then draws a picture of the scene, and compares illustrations with their peers.

Unit Book Clubs

Book Clubs are a great way to enhance class units or themes. For example, the following sequence can be used to develop five specialized clubs on the topic of food.

1. Preparation. First, select sets of texts that relate to the unit. Organize them around five loosely defined areas, in this instance: food preparation, cooking, shopping, healthy food, and snack food. Be sure each of these topics includes at least two book titles (see box for examples), which vary from high to low readability.

Sample Book Club Titles for a Unit on Food Study

Restaurant
Food Preparation
    Pritchett, Jan. *What Goes in a Salad?*, illustrated by Marjory Gardner. Crystal Lake, IL: Rigby, 1998.
    Pye, Trevor and Wilson, Cherry. *Pizza for Dinner*, illustrated by Trevor Pye. Crystal Lake, IL: Rigby, 1997.

Cooking
    Parker, John. *Dad Cooks Breakfast*, illustrated by Brent Putze. Crystal Lake, IL: Rigby, 1998.
    Pritchett, Jan. *In Norma's Kitchen*, photos by Malcolm Cross. Crystal Lake, IL: Rigby, 1998.

Shopping
    Cutting, Jillian. *Shopping*, photos by Fraser Newman. Bothell, WA: Wright Group, 1996.
    Heke, Carolyn. *Jack de Pert at the Supermarket*, illustrated by Trevor Pye. Bothell, WA: Wright Group, 1993.

Healthy Food
    Lockyer, John. *Carrots, Peas, and Beans*, illustrated by Lynn Breeze. Bothell, WA: Wright Group, 1996.
    McVeity, Jen. *Pop, Pop, Popcorn!* Illustrated by Trish Hill. Bothell, WA: Wright Group, 1998.

- Introduce the children to each of the books by "advertising" their contents. Once you've whetted their interest, place a copy of each of the books on the front chalk rail for perusal during the day.

- At the end of the day, have the children write down their first and second preferences for the topics they would like to explore.

2. Initial Club Meeting. The following day, assign children to one of the five Clubs, based on their topic choices.

- Before the clubs meet with their groups, have the class generate some ideas for how they'll conduct their meeting, including taking turns reading aloud, paired reading, and reading silently. Then each group chooses a format.

- Give each group a different graphic organizer to complete. (See sample reproducibles at end of chapter.) Use an overhead or large chart to model any of the unfamiliar materials.

- Have the groups find a comfortable spot in the room to begin reading one of their two titles. As they read, they complete their graphic organizer.

- Finally, have the children review their graphic organizers together and make any necessary changes.

3. Follow-Up Meeting. On the following day, the groups review the graphic organizer for the first book, and then read the second text.

- Remind the children to consider the first book as they are reading and think of ways that the two books are similar.

- The children then *synthesize* the similarities and use them as a springboard for a group poster illustrating information from both Book Club texts.

3. Final Session. As a concluding activity, have the Clubs take turns sharing their finished product. Group members can then place all Book Club titles in the Reading Corner for self-selected reading.

Whether it is through Strategy Circles, Learning Center activities, or Book Clubs, children's understanding of strategy use is enhanced as they share their thoughts with groups of peers who have similar abilities or interests. Strategy-focused instruction requires a mindful balance between implicit modeling interwoven throughout the day, and explicit instruction using texts that are at an individual child's instructional level. By combining just the right timing with just the right books, you can guide young children toward reaching their potential as proficient and enthusiastic readers.

STRATEGY CIRCLES

Dear Parents and Caregivers,

Reading-strategy instruction is integrated throughout your child's class work. Often, the whole class comes together while the teacher models new strategies that the children will practice independently later. However, strategy instruction through carefully planned, small-group, Strategy Circle activities is taking place every week.

Why small groups? While whole-group literacy instruction supports a collaborative classroom environment, using the same book to teach all children can be problematic. The material will bore some children, and others will find it too difficult. Small-group instruction gives each child the chance to practice strategies using texts selected specifically for his or her developmental level. Children learn best when they use books that are just right for them.

How are groups determined? Careful observation and informal assessments provide the information needed to develop appropriate Strategy Circle groupings. One assessment, Running Records, provides information on approximate reading levels. The Strategy Circle groups are reconfigured from time to time because every child develops at a different rate. In addition to Strategy Circles, your child will be part of Book Club groups, which are based on children's specific interests. These groups motivate children by encouraging them to share books and their own knowledge of classroom topics with their peers.

Why are small groups effective? Because they are based on your child's immediate needs and developmental level, small groups, such as Strategy Circles and Book Clubs, ensure that your child is receiving instruction using texts that are at just the right reading level. Strategy Circles also provide the best setting for explicit—or direct—instruction. A combination of indirect instruction, which often occurs during whole-class activities, and the explicit instruction during Strategy Circles provides your child with numerous opportunities to observe and practice a variety of strategies that will help him or her become a life-long reader!

Running Record Evaluation Sheet

Child's Name: _____   Date: _____

Text Title: _____   Level: _____

Word Analysis

No. of words _____ (1)

Words read incorrectly* – _____ (2)

= _____ (3)

(3)

___ X 100 = _____ % accuracy

(1)

100–95% accuracy = **Independence**
90–94% accuracy = **Instructional**
Below 90% = **Frustration**

***(Self-corrected words are NOT counted)**

Fluency

Dysfluent reading:

_____ Word-for-word reading

_____ Each word sounded out

························

Fluent reading:

_____ Appropriate intonation noted

_____ Character voices used

_____ Pauses at punctuation

	Word Analysis		
Miscue	Replaced By _____	Self-Corrected √	Omitted √

Strategies Observed

____ chunking	____ cross-checking	____ predicting
____ rereading	____ self-correcting	____ skipping
____ sliding	____ stretching	____ summarizing
____ thinking aloud	____ tracking	____ visualizing
____ _____	____ _____	____ _____

Teaching Reading Strategies in the Primary Grades Scholastic Professional Books

Strategy Interview

Child : _____   Date: _____

Part A: Pragmatics *[Three different text items from the classroom are presented to the child.]*

1. Here are some things from our classroom that you might read. How is reading (item #1) different from reading a book? Show me.

2. How is reading (item #2) different from reading a book? Show me.

3. What do you do *before* you read?

Part B: Grapho–Phonemics *[A book from the classroom is used for Parts B-D.]*

1. What do you do when you are reading and get stuck on a *word*? Show me.

2. How do you know when that word is fixed?

3. How does punctuation help you when you're reading? Show me.

Part C: Syntax

1. What do you do when you're reading and a *sentence* just doesn't sound right? Show me.

2. How do you know when that sentence is fixed?

Part D: Semantics

1. What do you do when you're reading and a *word* doesn't make sense? Show me.

2. What do you do when you're reading and you don't understand something in the *story*? Show me.

3. How do you know when it makes sense?

Final Question: Do you have any questions for me?

Strategy Circle Observation Form

Date:

Students:

Strategies Observed:

_____ predicting

_____ checking the picture

_____ tracking the words

_____ sliding to the end

_____ stretching the word

_____ finding chunks

_____ rereading

_____ cross-checking

_____ thinking aloud

_____ self-correcting

_____ _____

I= strategy introduced	R= strategy reviewed
M= teacher modeling of new strategy	P= plan for future ses-
sion	

Description of activities:

Observations:

Question Marker

Word-Level Questions	Text-Level Questions
How did the pictures help you figure out difficult words? *(checking)*	How does this story relate to something that has happened to you? *(activating)*
Show me a tricky word in this text. What chunks can you use to figure out this word? *(chunking)*	Who are the main characters in this story? *(analyzing)*
What Word Wall words did you find in this text? *(cross-checking)*	Where did the story take place? *(analyzing)*
Did rereading help you figure out any tricky words in this text? Show me. *(rereading)*	Can you tell me the major events in this story? *(analyzing)*
Were there any words that you went back to fix? *(self-correcting)*	What were the most important events or facts in this story? The least important? *(focusing)*
Which words did you skip over when you were reading? *(skipping)*	What do you think would happen next in this story if it continued? *(predicting)*
Which words did you slide through to figure them out? *(sliding)*	What questions did you ask yourself while you were reading? *(questioning)*
Show me a long word in this story. Can you stretch it out? *(stretching)*	What was this book about? *(summarizing)*
Were you able to follow all the words in this story? Show me. *(tracking)*	How is this story like another book you have read? *(synthesizing)*
What strategy was most useful to you to figure out tricky words?	Why did you choose this book? *(synthesizing)*
	What did you see in your mind while you were reading this book? *(visualizing)*

Fold Here

Fact Search

While I read . . . .
New facts I learned

Before I read . . . .
Things I want to know

Character Comparison

Character #1 _____	How They Are The Same	Character #2 _____

Story Strip Sequence

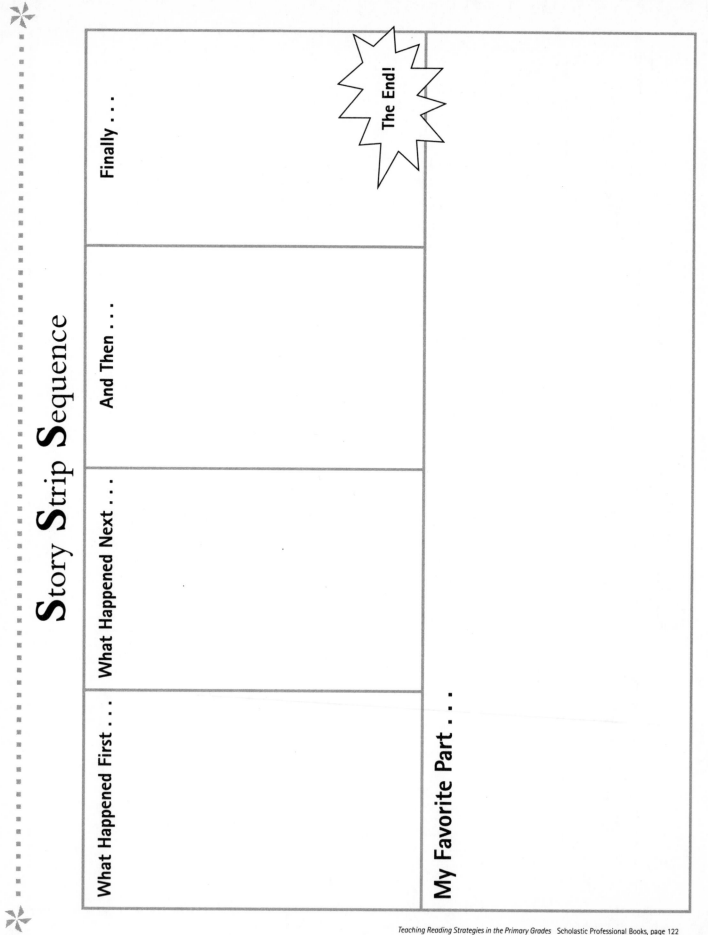

What Happened First . . .	What Happened Next . . .	And Then . . .	Finally . . .

The End!

My Favorite Part . . .

Word Web

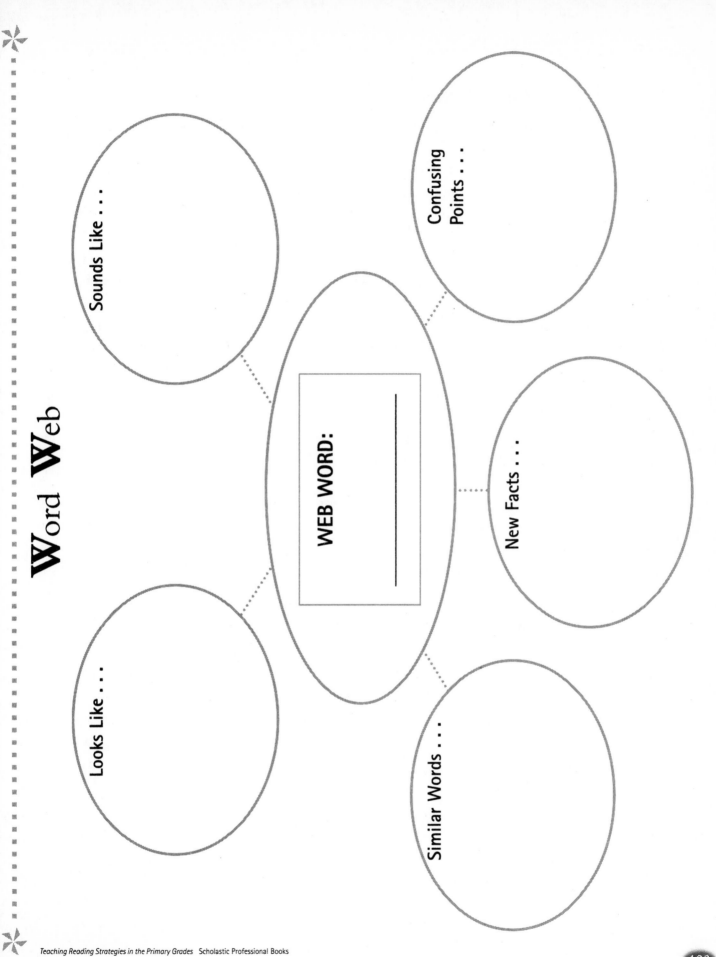

Sounds Like . . .

Confusing Points . . .

WEB WORD:

Looks Like . . .

New Facts . . .

Similar Words . . .

Chapter References

Burpo, D. C., and Wheeler, P. J. R. "Cooperative Learning Centers in an Inner City Classroom." *Teaching PreK-8*. 25 no. 1, (August/September, 1994): 76-78.

Campana, A. M., Pickenpaugh, L., Henry, J. M., and Wiley, B. J. *Teaching for Strategies in Guided Reading and Interactive Writing*. Research report presented at the International Reading Associate Annual Conference, Indianapolis, IN. (May, 2000).

Fawson, P. C., and Reutzel, D. R. "But I Only Have a Basal: Implementing Guided Reading in the Early Grades." *The Reading Teacher*. 54, no. 1 (September, 2000): 84-97.

Flood, J., Lapp, D., Flood, S., and Nagel, G. "Am I Allowed to Group? Using Flexible Patterns for Effective Instruction." *The Reading Teacher*. 45, no. 8 (April, 1992): 608-616.

Novelli, J. "Learning Centers that Work." *Instructor*. 105 no. 2 (September, 1995): 82-85.

Opitz, M. F. "Empowering the Reader in Every Child: The Case for Flexible Grouping When Teaching Reading." *Instructor*. 108, no. 5 (January/February, 1999): 35-38.

Patton, M. M., and Mercer, J. (1996). "'Hey! Where's the Toys?' Play and Literacy in the First Grade." *Childhood Education*. 73, no. 1 (Fall, 1996): 10-16.

Schulman, M. B., and Payne, C. D. *Guided Reading: Making It Work*. New York: Scholastic Professional Books, 2000.

Shea, M. *Taking Running Records*, Scholastic Professional Books, 2000.

Snowden, P. L., and Christian, L. G. (1998). "Four Levels of Learning Centers for Use with Young Gifted Children." *Gifted Child Today*. 21, no. 5 (September/October, 1998): 36-41.

Text-Level Strategies and Comprehension

Sharing the reading experience with others builds young children's text-level strategies—and confidence!

We've seen that a sense of community is important in creating the physical environment of the classroom, exploring ways to celebrate the uniqueness of each child, and establishing small-group sessions on strategies. In this chapter, we'll target the variety of ways to share authentic text across the whole learning community— emphasizing those strategies that focus on text-level comprehension.

Reading Aloud

Reading aloud to children is a critical component of early literacy instruction. As you immerse children in quality literature, you can demonstrate your own thinking processes by modeling and talking about the reading strategies you use. Read aloud sessions are particularly well suited for focusing on comprehension.

Reading Aloud

Reading aloud to young children is arguably the single most important activity for building the knowledge and skills needed to be a successful reader.

Reading aloud . . .

◆ significantly increases word knowledge and reading comprehension.

◆ motivates children to read on their own.

◆ provides access to new and interesting experiences.

◆ promotes imaginative thinking.

◆ develops listening skills.

Reading aloud also helps children gain in literacy development when you . . .

◆ choose books that are slightly above children's own reading level.

◆ use authentic literature.

◆ show illustrations as you read, modeling their importance as part of the text's meaning.

◆ use enlarged texts to increase children's awareness of the format and function of print.

◆ reread books to help children acquire sight words and draw them deeper into the text.

Reading aloud further provides instructional time for modeling . . .

◆ how good readers sound.

◆ specific comprehension strategies.

◆ how to analyze story structure.

◆ how to summarize the text.

◆ how to construct word meanings.

Reading aloud helps develop children's sense of self, as they compare their own experiences to those of the characters, respond to situations, and evaluate their feelings.

Sources: Adams, 1990; Coiro, 2000; Lacedonia, 1999; Ouellette, Dagostino, and Carifio, 1999.

▲ It's critical to read aloud every day in every classroom.

Planning for Daily Read Alouds

It's essential to read aloud to young children every day and to include both incidental (teachable moments) and directed sessions. When planning for Read Alouds . . .

✳ consider selecting books that relate to a current event or a unit the class is studying.

✳ make sure to use a variety of genres including fiction, traditional tales, nonfiction, and poetry.

✳ include time to reread books more than once.

✳ create an inviting environment.

A Typical Read Aloud Session

1. ***Introduce the story.*** Model the strategy of *predicting* by inviting students to guess what the book will be about as you review the title and cover illustrations. Take the class on a picture walk through the book's illustrations before they listen to the text.

   • Examples:

      Introduce David McKee's book, *Elmer*, (Lothrop, Lee, and Shepard, 1986) by bringing out and passing around a stuffed animal of Elmer.

      Introduce the book *Fire Fighters*, by Robert Maass (Scholastic, 1989), during a unit on fire safety. Explain that you "want to learn more" about this topic.

      During a polar unit, introduce your Read Aloud book by showing the location of the North and South Poles on the globe. Compare these locations to the children's home state and discuss possible differences between the Poles and the students' community.

2. *Read the story aloud.* As you read aloud, model strategies that you're currently emphasizing. For example, take advantage of rich illustrations to demonstrate how to *check* for picture clues in figuring out difficult terminology. Model as well the strategy of *rereading* for fluency and for making corrections when the text doesn't make sense.

- Examples:

    When you're reading *Fire Fighters*, have the class carefully study the illustrations to find out what a *turntable* is and how it is used.

    When you're reading *Thanksgiving Treat*, by Catherine Stock (Aladdin, 1990), suggest definitions for the words *veranda* and *shucking*.

3. *Wrap Up.* Conclude the read aloud session by *accessing* your own experiences and sharing their connections to this book or other texts you've read in class. These text-to-self and text-to-text links are important in generating meaning from reading. Also invite children to read the book on their own during Morning Work or Independent Reading. Because the text is now familiar and you've endorsed it, children are confidently drawn to rereading it independently.

- Examples:

    Share your own family traditions with the children, highlighting vocabulary that is related to your ethnic or cultural celebrations. Invite the children to do the same. Then create a class book on celebrations.

▲ The Share Chair builds confidence and fluency.

Creating a Share Chair

To involve young students more fully in the Read Aloud experience, create a community "Share Chair." Here children can sit and share self-selected favorite books with their classmates. Having this special chair is motivating and builds confidence. Hearing a book review from a peer can also pique other children's interest in reading that book. You can use any comfortable chair, or the children and their parents can become involved with creating the chair.

Share Chair

Invite children and their caregivers to become involved in creating a classroom Share Chair. You'll give the children a special sense of pride in their learning environment, and you'll emphasize to parents the importance of reading aloud to a young child's literacy development.

1. Open House Chairs

- Before the open house, obtain three to five inexpensive, plain chairs. (Consider donations from local businesses.)

- On the night of the open house, have available such craft supplies as paint, brightly colored fabric, beads, wooden scraps and glitter, to decorate the chairs.

- Have the adults and children work in teams to decorate the most imaginative chair. You might give the teams a theme, such as favorite book characters, habitats, or community landmarks, to guide their creations.

- Later in the year, invite caregivers to come and read their own favorite children's books in the newly decorated Share Chairs.

2. Pillowcase Chairs: Pillowcases, decorated using permanent or fabric markers, are an economical alternative to real chairs. Slip newly decorated cases over existing classroom chairs and voila! You have Share Chairs.

3. Chair Auction: As a fundraising opportunity at the end of the year, auction off the chairs or pillowcases. Use the donations to buy summer reading materials or books for the class.

4. Home Chairs: Invite family members to create a Share Chair at home with their children and make it a focal point for special adult-child shared reading. Suggest the possibility of decorating these around a theme—the child's heritage or special family hobbies and outings. Encourage the children to take pictures of their home Share Chair and put these in a classroom photo gallery.

☑ Share Chair Routine

Incorporate Share Chair sessions into the daily classroom routine. Every day have at least one student choose a book—either brought from home or from the classroom library—to share. By becoming an expert on favorite books and sharing them with classmates, children gain confidence and build on familiar concepts and strategies. Let the children choose from lots of ways to share:

◆ Read your favorite page.

◆ Explain why you chose this book.

Set up a routine for selecting Share Chair volunteers so that everyone will have a chance. For example, write the name of each student on a Popsicle stick and place the sticks in a jar. Each day randomly draw three names and give these children the option of sharing or having their names returned to the jar to be drawn at another time. Keep a record of who has shared and who has not.

◆ Take the class on a Picture Walk.

◆ Describe your favorite character(s).

◆ Tell about the most dramatic event in the book.

◆ Share new facts that you learned.

◆ Describe the story's setting.

◆ Explain how this story compares with experiences you've had.

Also encourage classmates to ask the Share Chair reader about his or her book. Prompt them to make a positive comment and then ask the question. This is a great way to explore the difference between a statement and a question. And often, the topics introduced in these discussions become the springboard for a whole-class unit.

▲ Whole-group sessions cultivate a sense of community.

Whole-Group Literature Sharing

One of the best ways to target comprehension strategies is to engage the whole class in exploring a text in depth. Make a point of sharing pieces of familiar literature that bridge content areas every day. Focus on and model a variety of strategies specifically aimed at text comprehension. Because it's comprehension—not individual letter-sound recognition—that is central to such strategy instruction, these shared experiences are crucial.

Whether you use poems, anthologies, or short texts, there are a variety of whole-group activities to reinforce a range of literacy strategies. For these lessons, have the children sit together on a comfortable rug so that each can easily see and interact with enlarged text.

Sharing Poems: They're Short and Imaginative

Poems are especially appropriate texts for group lessons for two reasons. Because they are short, they enable young children to be successful with a complete piece of text. Also, poems often include rich language patterns that you can use to model many different strategies.

Here's a short lesson you might use with the Mother Goose poem, *Rain, Rain, Go Away*.

1. Enlarge and laminate the poem and place it on an easel.

2. Invite the students to *visualize* the type of weather that the poem describes as you *track* the text with a magic wand.

3. Elicit students' descriptions of rainy weather as it is described in the poem.

4. Reinforce various print concepts. For example, ask students to circle the letter *R* in the poem.

5. *Cross check* for familiar sight words using the classroom Lightning or Star Words chart or the Word Wall.

✳ Poetry Activities

Activity—Chicken Soup

Strategies used: chunking, cross-checking, sliding, tracking

Emerging readers enjoy short poems that contain a predictable pattern or rhymes. A favorite book is *Chicken Soup with Rice* by Maurice Sendak (HarperCollins, 1962), a month-by-month collection of poems.

At the beginning of each month, use an enlarged edition of the book to share that month's poem with the class. Some of the poems in this collection provide a quick geography lesson, as the children eagerly *cross check* with the class globe to discover the poem's location. For example, April's poem invites children to "go away to far-off Spain and old Bombay." It's also easy to reinforce the word-level strategies, including *chunking* and *sliding* as you track the poems with a magic wand.

▲ Include favorite poems in Literacy Notebooks.

Whole-Group Poetry

The children are sitting in the reading corner around a large laminated version of the poem *Show Fish* by Shel Silverstein (HarperCollins, 1996). Melody accesses the children's prior knowledge about the topic of fishing by asking them for their own experiences. Students are quick to share their adventures, successes, and near-catches.

Melody begins, "Listen while I read this poem aloud. You can join in with me if you'd like." Melody slowly reads the poem, *tracking* the text with a magic wand. She then *rereads* the poem, and many children enthusiastically join in.

"I think I see some Word Wall words in this poem. Let's *cross check* and see."

"I see the word *a*!" Brieanne shouts out.

"Good job. Come on up and circle the word *a*."

Brieanne circles all of the letter *a*'s in the poem.

"You certainly found a lot of *a*'s, Brieanne. Let's go back and *reread* to see which ones are the letter *a* and which ones are the word *a*. Remember, the word *a* stands by itself."

Together, the class decides which are words, and Melody underlines the correct responses.

"I see the word *in*," announces Ryan.

"OK. Come on up and circle the word *in*."

Ryan circles the chunk */in/* in the word thing.

"That's good thinking, Ryan. You have found the chunk */in/*. Remember, though, a word stands by itself. Do you see the word *in*? Let's *reread* and see."

Ryan rereads the poem with Melody and shakes his head.

"That's OK, Ryan. Chunks are very helpful in learning new words. Good thinking!" Melody continues using the example of the chunk */it/* and the word *it*. Children volunteer to come up to the chart to underline the word *it*, *cross checking* with the Word Wall.

Melody then writes the word *fish* on a separate piece of chart paper. "What is this word? It was in the poem we just read."

The children respond in unison, "*Fish*!"

"Good. Let's think of other words that start with this same sound."

The children generate words such as *fox, fix, firefly, fingers, fudge bar, fire, flash, flubber,* and *fashion*. Melody writes their suggestions, and then, as the children say each word again, one child comes up to the easel to underline the onset */f/*.

"You've done a super job today! Let's finish by *rereading* our new fishing poem together."

Activity—Poetry Keepers

Strategies used: previewing, visualizing

At the beginning of the year, have each child bring in an empty three-ring binder—now a Literacy Notebook—to hold poems as well as Special Person pieces (see Chapter 2). Store the notebooks in a large plastic tub in the reading corner.

Before you read a new poem, have class *preview* the text. Then, ask the children to close their eyes and listen as you read the poem to *visualize* what it's about. What image comes to mind? *Visualization* helps children focus on meaning in text, make connections with their own experiences, and stimulate their imaginative thinking. Here's how the lesson might go:

TEACHER TIP

You can use adopted basal series or anthologies for shared-group sessions. Just be sure to choose stories that your students find engaging and that fit the theme, unit, or concept you're teaching.

1. After you've shared the poem as a class, give the children copies to put in their Literacy Notebooks.

2. Have them draw what they visualized on their copy of the poem.

3. Next, the children should explore a variety of print concepts with individual poems (circle all of the Word Wall words, underline the proper nouns, and so on).

4. Finally, the children file the poem their Notebooks for later reference during Morning Work or Independent Reading.

5. As students collect a number of poems, have them create their own Table of Contents so they can easily access their favorites.

❋ More Whole-Group Activities

When you're sharing literature, provide lots of opportunities for children to engage with the text and with a Toolbox of comprehension strategies. Also encourage them to take class texts home where they can further explore these familiar books. Here's a sample lesson using *Silly Sally* by Audrey Wood (Harcourt, Brace, Jovanovich, 1992) that illustrates how you can get the children involved during a whole-group reading session. (See Chapter Two for a *Silly Sally* Chit-Chat activity.)

Silly-Sally-Story-Sequence Lesson

Day One: Introduce the story *Silly Sally* and *access* students' prior knowledge.

- Share something silly that has happened to you and invite students to share their own silly tales.

- After *checking* the cover title and illustrations and making *predications* about the book, take the children on a Picture Walk through the story.

- Read the story aloud to the class as you *track* the text. After discussing what the story was about, invite the children to use the Word Wall to *cross check* familiar words they find in the story.

Day Two: *Reread* the text, focusing on story vocabulary and concepts.

- As the class reads aloud together, again *track* the text.
- Ask the children to point out any difficult words in the story. *Check* the text illustrations and find *chunks* to learn the new vocabulary.
- Ask the children to *analyze* the story by sharing how this tale is the same, or different, from other silly stories they have recently read.

Day Three: Review the story and build on text-level strategy use.

- Ask the children to review the story by whispering their favorite part to their neighbor.
- Have the children listen to the story on tape while they follow along in their own books.
- Discuss the use of character voices on the tape and how they contribute to the text's meaning.
- *Summarize* the story by creating a flow chart of events using large sentence strips. Rearrange the flowchart as you add new ideas into the sequence.

Day Four: Have the children form pairs and *reread* the story together.

- Each child selects his or her favorite silly character and makes a simple puppet out of a paper bag.
- The pair then *rereads* the story using their puppets.
- Have the children put their individual text copies in a bag, along with a note to their caregivers, to be taken home and *reread* over the weekend.

Day Five: Extend the shared-reading experience.

- Review the story using the enlarged version of the book and *analyze* the story's predictable-language pattern.
- Together, generate a *Silly-Sally* book to publish and add to the classroom library.

You can easily use this sequence for many stories. We've included a variety of other whole-group activities starting on page 135.

Book Bags

Whenever multiple copies of a shared-reading book are available (including literature-based basals), routinely send them home for *rereading*. Place them in large, plastic zipper bags along with a letter, such as the one below explaining, which strategies you're focusing on or which Word Wall words you're emphasizing. Also include materials such as:

◆ a copy of the cumulative Word Wall words

◆ a portable Strategy Chart

◆ a Strategy Bookmark

◆ a log for family members to use as they note the child's progress.

Dear Caregiver,

This week we have been reading the story, *I Went Walking*, by Sue Williams (Harcourt, Brace, Jovanovich, 1989). This book has a predictable word pattern. As you are reading the story with your child, ask him or her to point out the pattern. When you are finished, write your own story together featuring new animals and your own child as the main character! Don't forget to turn in this signed note and the book on Monday.

Word Wall words: *did, I, me, see, we, went, what*

We have read this story together.

Caregiver's Signature _____ Child's Signature _____ Date _____

Activity—Cover Up

Strategies used: checking, questioning, skipping, thinking aloud, tracking

Using small sticky notes, cover up selected words in an enlarged book. Choose words that students can readily guess from picture clues or the context of the sentence. For younger readers, don't cover up more than one word in a sentence. As the children listen carefully, *track* the entire text first. Then, reread the text, pausing at the words you've covered up. *Think aloud* as you model how to use appropriate strategies for figuring out the word. Does it help to *check* picture clues? Also model how you use *questioning* to monitor your progress with the text.

Variation:

To demonstrate the strategy of *skipping* troublesome words, cover up some words that don't affect the text's meaning. For example, in the sentence, *I saw some squirrels run up the _____ tree*, the omitted word (*gnarly*) won't change the reader's understanding of this text. Discuss how sometimes it's fine to omit a word and continue reading in order to keep the flow and avoid missing the overall meaning of the story.

Activity—Character Comparisons

Strategies used: accessing, checking, predicting

Introduce the children to the *accessing* strategy by discussing a character in a story who has had similar experiences to the children's own, or by describing what they might have done if they had faced a similar situation. *Checking* picture clues is an interesting strategy for understanding characters' feelings or motivations. For example, invite the children to look carefully at picture illustrations for characters' facial expressions and *predict* what might happen with the character later in the story.

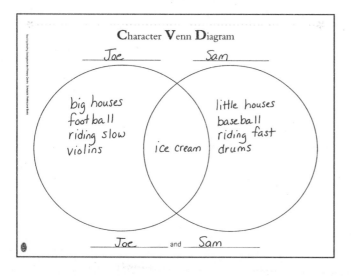

Activity—Character Comparisons

Strategies used: accessing, checking, predicting

As children become comfortable with concrete character comparisons, introduce the more abstract concept of comparing two fictional story characters. For example, in the story *How Joe the Bear and Sam the Mouse Got Together* by Beatrice DeRegniers (Lothrop, Lee, and Shepard, 1990), students can compare the friends Joe and Sam. Display a large Venn diagram for reference when you *reread* the story. Use character graphics as a reminder of the diagram's organization. (A reproducible is provided at the end of the chapter.)

While children listen to the story, they focus on what makes the characters different and what makes them similar. Add their observations to the chart. After you reread the story again, have the children *summarize* it using the clues on the diagram. Using the *analyzing* strategy will enhance students' understanding of the story's structure and meaning.

Activity—Character Puppets

Strategies used: analyzing, summarizing

Creating their own story puppets taps young children's artistic and kinesthetic abilities and builds text-level strategies such as summarizing and analyzing. Each child can either make his or her own complete set of puppets or can select individual characters. The children follow along and manipulate their puppets to match the action while you read the story aloud. As they become more comfortable with the story's sequence, small groups or pairs can reenact the story.

Puppets with Character

Chit Chat Puppets. Combine character puppets with a take-home, Chit Chat activity. (See page 52.) For example, children can make paper bag puppets for Don Freeman's bear character *Corduroy* (Viking, 1976) at home. Encourage them to be creative in designing overalls for their puppet. They might use cloth, buttons, fabric, and paper. Back at school, the children enjoy sharing their creations and using their new puppets during a *rereading* of the story.

Patterned Puppets. With stories that are highly patterned, like *Henny Penny* by Paul Galdone (Houghton Mifflin, 1984) or *The Napping House* by Audrey Wood (Harcourt, Brace, Jovanovich, 1984), create character cut-outs from scanned text images. On sentence-strip cards, write corresponding action words or sentences. Line up the characters on a pocket chart, and have students take turns matching selected action words (*snoozing*) with the character (*cat*).

Sequenced Puppets. Use character cutouts (attach magnetic strips to the back) to review highly sequenced stories, like *I Went Walking*, by Sue Williams (Harcourt, Brace, Jovanovich, 1989). Have the children line up the characters in the order they appear in the story on a pocket chart or a magnetized white board. Draw a simple map of the story's setting on butcher paper to use as a backdrop.

Activity—Story Spin

Strategies used: analyzing, previewing

Use a Story Spin either as a whole-group activity or as a Learning Log (Chapter 4) project. After reading a story, introduce the activity to the class by displaying a large divided circle with the sections: *characters*, *setting*, *events*, and *story ending*. (See reproducible at end of chapter.) With a brad fastener, attach an arrow to

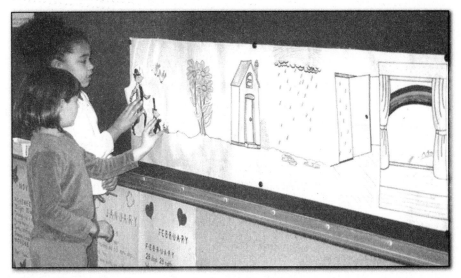

▲ Children build story-comprehension skills with creative character maps.

the center of a laminated copy of the circle. Have children take turns spinning the arrow and then describing that element of the story that the arrow landed on. For example, if it lands on *events*, the child would describe one event in the story. You can write the response on the laminated circle or attach a sticky note. The next child then takes a turn and adds new information to what others have shared.

Variations:

◆ Use the Spin to introduce the story and model the strategy of *previewing*.

◆ Have students paste a blank Spin sheet into their Learning Logs and *analyze* the story by writing or drawing descriptions of the book's characters, events, setting, and ending.

◆ Add different sections, such as *my reaction* or *new facts*, to customize the activity.

Activity—Flowcharts

Strategies used: cross-checking, summarizing

Create individual cards or strips that describe separate story events. For example, after reading the story, *The Chick and the Duckling* by Mirra Ginsburg (Macmillan, 1972), you'd make the following cards:

◆ Duckling and Chick come out of their shells.

◆ They take a walk.

◆ They dig holes.

◆ They find a worm.

◆ They catch butterflies.

◆ They go for a swim.

◆ Duckling pulls out Chick.

◆ Duckling jumps in the water.

◆ Chick says, "Not me!"

Pass out the sequence cards to the children, who are seated at their tables or in groups. Give each group one to three cards, depending on the summary's length. As a team, the group reads their cards and decides whether they have the sentence that should come first in the story's sequence. If they do, they tape it onto a class chart, where it's followed by the remaining sentences. As each new event is added, draw arrows between the cards to illustrate the flow of the story. Read the completed flowchart as a final summary and double check on story sequence. As children become more familiar with flowcharts, you can develop a variety of small group and individualized activities.

Expansions ◆◆◆◆◆◆◆◆◆◆◆◆◆◆◆◆◆◆◆◆

Flowcharts

Flowcharts provide children of all ages and levels with a concrete way to visualize and *summarize* a story.

Nonfiction Flowcharts: Fiction flowcharts are most common, but the charts work well for nonfiction, too. A flowchart can summarize a text that describes a tree's life cycle or the passing seasons. More proficient readers will discover that flowcharts are not always linear. When they create a flowchart to illustrate the life cycle of a tree or flower, for example, they'll see that the death of the plant circles back to new life as a seed is planted and germinates.

Graphic Flowcharts: For very young children, use graphics to introduce flowcharts. For example, after hearing the classic children's story *Millions of Cats* by Wanda Ga'g (Scholastic, 1956), show the children pictures (scanned from the illustrations) that show important events in the story. Discuss what each picture represents. Then scramble the pictures and have children take turns putting them back in order. Finally, give the children their own copies of the story- event pictures to color, order, and put together as their own book.

Summary Flowcharts: Proficient readers can use flowcharts in a variety of ways and with deepening sophistication. For example, children can create their own individual-ized flowcharts to describe the events that they believe are most pivotal to the text. Students can then compare flowcharts with peers to determine which events the majority of their classmates felt were most important. When they're reading longer stories or novels, students can create charts for each chapter and then develop a final chart that illustrates how events throughout the book are interconnected.

"What-If?" Flowcharts: First, have the children create a linear flowchart to summarize a story's major points. Then ask them to create branches describing what might have happened if a character had made a different decision. Here's an example from the tale *Tacky the Penguin* by Helen Lester (Houghton Mifflin, 1988).

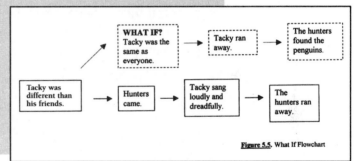

Figure 5.5. What If Flowchart

Try the following activities, which can be used in a variety of small or paired groupings, to extend whole-group reading experiences—and strategy use.

Activity—Sticky Note Reading

Strategies used: analyzing, confirming, cross-checking, synthesizing

Give each pair or group a sticky note marked with a different comprehension concept to attend to while rereading. For example, you may ask Brittany and Jill to find a description of the main character, while Josh and Mike are to find the passage that best describes the story's setting.

As the pairs reread, they *analyze* the text for their assigned concept. When they've found it, they place their note on that page for reference. The pair continues to read in order to *confirm* their selection. When all of the pairs have read the story, gather the class together to *synthesize* their findings. When questions or possible discrepancies arise, use the text to *cross check* responses.

Activity—Puzzle Pieces

Strategies used: analyzing, cross-checking

One creative way to engage children in reviewing strategies is through a "puzzling" activity. First, select four to six simple puzzles with large pieces. Before the class session, write text-level questions on the back of each puzzle—a different question per piece. So that the puzzles can be used for more than one session, make questions general rather than specific to one book or piece of literature. For example, the question "What is the most important point in this story?" would be more appropriate than, "What did Samuel do after he was lost?"

After you share and *reread* a text, give each group or pair the puzzle pieces to a complete puzzle. Have the children take turns selecting a puzzle piece and *analyzing* the text to answer the question. When discrepancies arise between a child's response and that of his or her peers', the children can *cross check* it with the story. As each puzzle question is answered, the piece is turned over. When all of the questions are answered, the group collaboratively completes the puzzle picture.

Author Studies

The whole-group setting is perfect for sharing books by a favorite author or based on a central theme. Series texts like the *Arthur* books by Marc Brown (Little Brown, 1983, 1984, 1985, 1996) or the classic tales of Ezra Jack Keats (Aladdin, 1987, 1987, 1998) work very well.

With a unifying theme or books by one author, children can:

✳ explore common textual patterns or illustrative styles.

✳ trace the development of reccurring characters and study their traits in more depth.

✳ learn more about the writing process through the eyes and words of published writers.

Children can also access information about authors and illustrators via educational Web sites.

☑ Spotlight on Seuss

Readers at all levels enjoy the rich language of Dr. Seuss (whose texts are particularly appropriate for Book Clubs—see Chapter 4). His books can be categorized in a variety of ways:

◆ **Patterned Texts.** Classic books like *One Fish, Two Fish* (Random House, 1960) and *Green Eggs and Ham* (Random House, 1960) support emerging readers with their repetitive patterns and predictable rhymes. The books are also excellent for developing phonemic awareness. Because of their patterns in onsets and rimes, they provide rich opportunities for modeling the *chunking* and *sliding* strategies.

Ways to use Norman Bridwell's *Clifford* Books for Learning and Fun

◆ Wear red (Clifford's favorite color!)

◆ Chart favorite Clifford stories

◆ Search for author information on the Internet

◆ Write a new Clifford adventure

◆ Make character masks and recreate the story through Readers' Theater

◆ Have a pet day at school

◆ Adopt a class pet

◆ Study different breeds of dogs

◆ Make a life-sized poster of Clifford

◆ Compare Clifford's measurements with those of real dogs

◆ Write about your own experiences with pets

◆ Hold a dog-biscuit sale to raise money for the Humane Society

◆ Study the role of dogs through history

◆ Learn about famous dogs or pets of famous people

◆ Write a letter to a presidential pet

◆ Write a birthday song for Clifford

◆ Hold a birthday party—with red punch and bone-shaped cookies

◆ **Thematic Texts.** Because of its tie to the timely issue of environmental science, an extended focus on *The Lorax* (Random House, 1971) is appropriate for all young readers. Children apply the *questioning* strategy as they discuss the impact their own decisions make on their community and surrounding environment. In small groups, they can write new story endings to be laminated and bound as a class book.

◆ **Current Events.** Seuss explores sophisticated societal themes in books like *The Butter Battle* (Random House, 1984), which focuses on the build up towards war, and *The Sneetches* (Random House, 1961), which targets the ever-timely issue of accepting differences. These are appropriate for more proficient readers, who can access their own world experiences and *analyze* the ideas portrayed in the books.

Here are some ways to immerse students in the world of Dr. Seuss. You can adapt these ideas for any other favorite author:

◆ Decorate the room with posters or books jackets illustrative of Dr. Seuss's creations.

◆ Make large paper Cat in the Hat hats to wear while you share new Dr. Seuss books.

◆ After reading several Dr. Seuss books, create a chart illustrating some of the favorites.

◆ When Dr. Seuss's birthday arrives in March, celebrate with a cat-shaped cake.

◆ Invite children's family members into class to read their favorite Dr. Seuss tales.

Paired Reading—For Fluency

▲ Shoebox sharing provides an interactive review of familiar texts.

We've explored a variety of ways to share quality literature with emerging readers and at the same time model and explicitly teach the use of strategies in the context of authentic text. However, children also need time to practice and apply these strategies individually and with their peers in an environment that encourages risk-taking with print. By rereading familiar and predictable texts, for example, young children will build both confidence and fluency in their own reading. We've found that one of the best types of paired reading strategies for enhancing young children's fluency is to incorporate Shoebox activities.

What the Experts Say About . . .

Fluency

If children can't read fluently, they can't understand what they read.

Fluency is the ability to read text rapidly, effortlessly, and automatically. Fluent readers do not have to consciously attend to such reading mechanics as decoding, sounding out, or phrasing. They do it naturally; and therefore they are able to focus on the meaning of the text.

Dysfluent readers have difficulty understanding what is being read because they must focus on small units of language, such as isolated sounds. Dysfluency is one of the most common characteristics of struggling readers and can adversely affect motivation and reading proficiency.

Teachers can support their students' fluency development by modeling what words in print should sound like when they are read. Reading aloud is critical for any classroom. In addition, teachers should provide access to a variety of familiar and easy texts so that students can practice independent reading successfully.

The effects of repeated readings can be powerful. Rereading can improve fluency, accuracy, expression, word recognition, vocabulary, and comprehension. Rereading can also deepen students' interpretations of texts and help them make connections from the printed page to their own lives.

Sources: Mastropieri, Leinart, and Scruggs, 1999; Meyer and Felton, 1999; Rasinski and Padak, 2000; Schulman and Payne, 2000; Tompkins, 1997.

Shoebox Reading

With the Shoebox strategy, children read from an expanding collection of short, predictable texts kept in individual shoeboxes. Such activities begin with the whole group and lead to paired readings that, by providing strategy practice, build confidence and fluency. Here's how to set up for Shoeboxes activities.

1. **Preparing the Shoeboxes.** Locate containers that can hold texts approximately the size of a half sheet of paper. Some possibilities:

   • Clean, cardboard shoeboxes.

   • Modified cereal boxes with the box top cut open.

   • Small plastic utility boxes (the sturdiest option).

   • Label the boxes with the children's names (one name per box) and shelve them for easy access.

2. **Selecting Texts.** Since Shoebox activities are designed to develop fluency, select texts that are generally at or slightly below the class reading level. Common resources include:

   • short, reproducible texts. These are widely available through teacher resource stores and are also often included in classroom literature series and teaching magazines. (A list of possible sources is included in the Professional Resources Appendix at the back of this book.)

   • simple, patterned student-created texts.

   • stories from discarded basals, cut out and stapled as booklets

Send-Home Ideas ■ ■ ■ ■ ■ ■ ■ ■ ■ ■ ■ ■ ■ ■ ■ ■

Discarded Treasures

Invite caregivers to help create booklets for classroom Shoeboxes.

✳ Send students home with a copy of a discarded basal and directions for which stories to select (or, ask students and their families to choose their favorites).

✳ Instruct students and their caregivers to cut or tear the stories from the basal and staple each one into an individual booklet.

✳ Encourage families to use construction paper or file folders to create imaginative covers for the booklets.

✳ After they practice reading the stories at home, students are ready to add these "discarded treasures" to their classroom Shoeboxes.

3. **Shared Reading.** After selecting a text to be used for the Shoebox activity, give each child his or her own copy. Introduce the story to the whole class. Then read it chorally together with the children, who should be *tracking* in their own copies.

4. **Paired Reading.** With their Shoeboxes in hand, have student pairs find comfortable spots around the classroom for reading. Rotate pairs frequently to allow students to build friendships with many classmates. Provide about 10 minutes for paired-reading activities at the beginning of the year. Increase the time as the year and text level progress. Have the pairs begin by *rereading* the day's newly introduced story. They can choose either to read it together or take turns reading aloud. Finally, encourage them to delve into the Shoebox to revisit old favorites.

5. **Shoebox Assessment.** You can capitalize on Shoebox partner time to observe how students are using strategies and, in particular, how fluent they are with familiar text. Make note of students who are struggling and adjust subsequent lessons appropriately.

✳ Shoebox Activities

If you supplement commercially prepared booklets with teacher-created texts, you can make them specific to the needs of your students. The following activities can be used in specializing the Shoebox experience.

Create Shoebox–Activity Booklets With These Stems

Replicate any or all of the following stems to create separate Shoebox booklets. Be sure each booklet contains at least six pages of the same stem. The repetition inherent in each of these booklets, which build on key sight words, develops fluency and familiarity with the text pattern. They help emerging readers acquire print concepts and attend to text.

1. Here is the __(object)__ .
2. I see a __(classroom object)__ .
3. I can help __(family member)__ .
4. I can play with __(toy)__ .
5. Do you like __(sport)__ ? Yes or no?
6. Where is the __(school object)__ ? Here is the __(object)__ .
7. What said __(animal sound)__ ? The __(animal)__ said __(sound)__ .
8. I will eat __(food)__ .
   FINAL PAGE: But I will not eat __(food)__ .
9. I can have a pet __(animal)__ .
   FINAL PAGE: I cannot have a pet __(animal)__ .

Activity—I Can _____ Booklist

Strategies used: checking, tracking

"I Can" booklets focus on reviewing sight vocabulary. Using large font in a simple word processing program, type "*I can _____ and _____*" on half sheets of paper. Give each child six sheets of the same sentence stem, stapled at the side. In addition, for each child prepare a sheet of computer-generated pictures depicting children engaged in a variety of activities (including reading, of course!). See the sample "I Can_____" booklet reproducible at the end of this chapter.

Pattern for "I Can" Booklet

I can _____ and _____ .

1. Write the *I can _____ and _____* sentence stem on the board and review it with the class. *Track* the text as the class repeats the sentence chorally.

2. Review the picture prompts to clarify different interpretations of the illustrations.

3. Students next select pictures to represent some of their favorite activities and cut and paste them into their own booklets. In this way, they are *checking* the picture to make meaning with print.

Activity—Color Booklets

Strategies used: tracking, visualizing

Shoebox booklets are great for practicing color and number concepts. Students particularly enjoy an activity centered on the poetry book, *Hailstones and Halibut Bones* by Mary O'Neill (Doubleday, 1989). Read selected color poems from this engaging book and have the children visualize to bring the poems alive. Then explain to students that they can create their own color books. They'll focus on one color a day until there are six pages.

1. **Color Walk.** On your students' first color book day, take a quick Color Walk in the classroom, paying special attention to the day's focus color—let's say green. Afterwards, students brainstorm a list of green items—*leaves, apples, grass, books, moss, scissors, go lights, pickles, bushes, celery, grasshoppers*. Write these on the chalkboard with green chalk

2. **Color Selection.** Invite students to select those items that are green *all the time*. Mark these with a star.

3. **Color De-Selection.** When the always-green list is completed, have the class brainstorm items that are never green—*sky, snow, pigs, sun, moon, elephants, blackbirds*. Write these on the chalkboard with white chalk.

4. **Color Sentences.** Distribute a small sheet of green construction paper with the

following sentences:

A _____ is green.

A _____ is green.

A _____ is green.

But a _____ is never green.

Based on the class lists, or their own imaginations, students complete their color page. Continue on subsequent days with red, yellow, blue, orange, and purple.

Variations:

◆ When the six pages are complete, bind each booklet for the children's Shoeboxes.

◆ Use the booklets as part of a mini-lesson on the *tracking* strategy. Model how to track each word as you reread the stem, pausing at the color words. Ask students to count how many color words appear on each page, and have them circle these in their own booklets.

Activity—Sticker Zoo Booklets

Strategies used: building fluency, forming sounds

This activity is for children who are still developing early-literacy concepts. It focuses on category-specific vocabulary in a rebus-like format that minimizes the amount of text. For example, provide each child with stickers based on a selected category of common items (*animals*, *food*, or *seasons*, for example) and a six-page Shoebox booklet each with the simple stem:

A _____.

Have the children place one sticker per page on the blank. For a zoo booklet, for instance, a child might select a sticker of a *giraffe*, an *elephant*, a *monkey*, a *bear*, a *tiger*, and a *lion*. Bind the books, and young children can immediately "read" their special text. This activity works very well with very young learners. The children have a successful experience with print and develop early-strategy use in *building fluency* and *forming sounds*.

Variations:

◆ Write the name of the animal under each sticker.

◆ Encourage the children to complete the sentence with an action word. (For example, *The monkey climbs.*)

◆ Add background illustrations.

◆ As a follow-up Chit Chat activity, ask children and their caregivers to add new animals and actions to this special Sticker Zoo.

Activity—Nursery Rhyme Booklets

Strategies used: analyzing, rereading, self-correcting, tracking

Create Nursery Rhyme booklets by reproducing from the variety of widely available commercial formats. The predictability of many of these texts makes them perfect for fostering students' confidence and fluency. In addition, the unusual vocabulary in many of the pieces offers a challenge for more able readers. These booklets allow readers to expand their strategy repertoire from *tracking* and *rereading* to the more complex use of context to analyze the tales' vocabulary. It's easy to modify the following plan, based on *Diddle, Diddle, Dumpling*, for any traditional rhyme.

> Diddle, diddle dumpling,
> My son John
> Went to bed with his britches on;
> One shoe off, the other shoe on,
> Diddle, diddle dumpling,
> My son John

1. Read the rhyme with an enlarged version, modeling the *tracking* and *self-correcting* strategies.

2. Invite the children to *track* and *reread* the verse in their own booklets.

3. To review sight vocabulary, have the students locate and circle the word *my* on the first page of the booklet. Then have them independently find and circle any *my's* they discover on the remaining pages.

4. Repeat this process for any targeted sight words as students identify subsequent vocabulary with squares, stars, or dots.

5. Introduce the children to some of the unusual vocabulary often found in this traditional genre

Expansions ◆◆◆◆◆◆◆◆◆◆◆◆◆◆◆◆◆◆◆

Word Wizards

Besides increasing the complexity of the texts chosen for the Shoebox collections, encourage more proficient readers to stretch their abilities through extended concept activities. The Word Wizard activity in particular is well suited for nursery rhymes, which often contain antiquated but alluring vocabulary.

1. Invite students to highlight any unfamiliar vocabulary in a newly introduced nursery rhyme. The words *dumpling* and *britches* are two examples found in the verse *Diddle Diddle Dumpling*.

2. Have the class use context clues to *think aloud* about the verse and *predict* what the words mean.

3. The whole class or small research teams then craft definitions. You may want to model dictionary use as a resource. Chart and display final responses for reference.

Tricky Word	What I think it means (prediction)	What it really means	Where I found the answer

Further extensions of the Word Wizard include:

✳ Have students record the definition and source of the terms they find to be most intriguing in individual Word Wizard lists or glossaries.

✳ Incorporate new terms into creative new tales or rhymes.

✳ Reproduce these original tales for each class member's Shoebox.

Activity—Sequence Booklets

Strategies used: confirming, summarizing, visualizing

You can develop sequencing activities with a variety of texts. The following example relies on the book *Corduroy* by Don Freeman (Viking, 1976), but you can incorporate the ideas into other shared-book experiences.

◆ **Chart the Sequence.** After reading this favorite tale aloud, invite the children to summarize the sequence of the story's events and chart their responses. For example, students might generate the following sentences:

1. Lisa wanted Corduroy, but her Mom said not today.

2. He climbed off his shelf to find his button.

3. He rode up an escalator.

4. Corduroy fell asleep.

◆ **Confirm the Sequence.** Have the class reread the chart as you hold up corresponding illustrations in the book. This allows the students to *confirm* their sequencing.

◆ **Create Sequence Booklets.** On a subsequent day, distribute prepared booklets—one sentence to a page—of the students' story sequence. Reread both the chart and the booklet.

◆ **Add Illustrations.** Guide students to use the booklet's sentence prompts *to visualize* and illustrate the story event on each page. The booklets can be added to students' Shoeboxes.

Variation:

◆ Invite students to create a brief class summary of a story they have read. As students suggest ideas, write summary sentences on long strips of paper. Have the class reread the sentences together in the correct order to create a chart-sized summary that includes each of the strips.

◆ Working in small groups or pairs, students write individual summary sentences on an 8½" x 11" sheet cut into three to five strips. Next, students exchange and sequence each other's strips. Finally have them glue their individual strips onto construction paper in the correct sequence. Later students can illustrate their summaries and add them to their Shoeboxes.

TEACHER TIP

Because Shoebox collections are so popular with students, they can rapidly expand and eventually outgrow their containers. At least twice a year, have students select two to four favorite texts to keep as part of their classroom Shoebox collection. Send the remaining pieces home to put in Family Shoeboxes, where they can be collected, reread, and enjoyed.

Independent Reading

A quiet hum greets a visitor to Melody's classroom during the children's favorite Book Basket activity. In the center of each table a plastic basket overflows with a variety of texts and print materials. Timon and Samuel are searching through one basket together. Timon selects *Tacky the Penguin* by Helen Lester (Houghton Mifflin, 1988), a book that Melody read aloud to the class the week before. He settles back into his chair and begins a picture walk to review the story. At another table, Lis excitedly reviews a treasure-hunt brochure that Bette had brought back from a recent trip to Arizona. Melody, seated at a back table, listens as Jose shares his favorite part of the book, *Who Is the Beast?* by Keith Baker (Harcourt, Brace, Jovanovich, 1990). Both remark on the use of brilliant colors in the bold illustrations.

While whole- and small-group activities support children in learning and practicing new strategies, daily independent reading of self-selected books is critical to their continuing growth in applying these strategies. Children eagerly practice using comprehension-level strategies when they get to choose books they most *want* to read. Therefore, strategies-focused teachers need to fill the classroom with terrific books at a range of levels, topics, and genres.

Book Baskets

One of the ways to make sure that children have access to a variety of books is to create a Book Basket (or plastic tub) for each group or table in the classroom. Rotate the baskets once a week. Baskets should include:

◆ books representing many reading levels.

◆ different types of text, such as environmental print, magazines, poems, and class-created pieces.

▲ Book Baskets offer a variety of texts for independent reading.

◆ texts that relate to a current theme or are written by an author you're studying.

◆ children's strategy bookmarks (see Chapter 4, page 119), which encourage applying new strategies to independent reading.

Consider sharing Book Baskets between grade-level classrooms to provide children with access to an even wider array of texts.

☑ Introducing Book Baskets

It's important to model the process of self selecting books, particularly at the beginning of the year or with very young readers. Demonstrate how to *preview* a book by checking out the cover, reading the title, walking through the story illustrations, and reading the first few pages. And be sure to model the importance of finding a book that's at just the right level—not so easy that it's boring, but not so difficult that meaning is lost. Have children serve as models for their peers by explaining how they've selected a good book. One way to get students excited about reading something new is to "advertise" new materials before you put them in Book Baskets.

CHECKING UP ON LEARNING ▶

Reading Conferences

You can incorporate many types of reading conferences into a strategies-centered classroom and gain a depth of information through careful observation. As you meet individually with the children, you can ask each child to:

✳ read his or her favorite part of the story.

✳ use the pictures to describe a favorite or compelling event.

✳ compare his or her own experiences with those portrayed in the story.

✳ compare the story with other stories already read.

✳ point out difficult words and describe what strategies he or she used to figure them out.

Here are two ideas for *tracking* students' progress over time.

✳ **Record Ring:** Use a ring of index cards—one per student—to jot down anecdotal notes.

✳ **Observation Form:** Create a simple form to record your observations. (See reproducible at end of chapter.) As noted on the sample, the form focuses on strategy use, comprehension, and fluency.

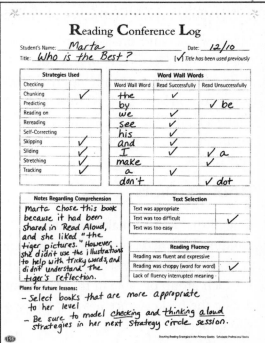

▲ Reading Conferences provide valuable information about each child's strategy use.

Conferencing

Ongoing conferencing is essential for keeping a close watch on students' progress and for providing the right subsequent lessons at the opportune time. Through these one-on-one exchanges, teachers can . . .

♦ informally assess how the child comprehends text or is processing print.

♦ determine which strategies the child is using.

♦ note the child's problem-solving abilities, fluency rate, and print-to-text connections.

♦ identify what each child knows and what he or she needs in subsequent lessons.

♦ introduce or reteach a specific strategy.

♦ model excitement and engagement with print.

Here are some tips for conducting successful conferences:

♦ Establish a predictable time for conferences. They can be as short as one minute or as long as the schedule and child's needs allow.

♦ Have students begin by talking about what they've read, retelling the story, or reading a favorite part aloud.

♦ Provide support by demonstrating or suggesting strategies at the point of need or simply by sharing your own experiences with that text.

Sources: Dahl, Schaver, Lawson, and Grogan, 1999; Five and Dionisio, 1998; Gill, 2000; Manning, 1998.

☑ Book Basket Conferences

During the time children are independently exploring their Book Basket treasures, you have a great opportunity to conference and assess how well they're doing at using specific strategies. Administer monthly Running Records (see Chapter 4) during this time or conduct five-minute, informal student-teacher conferences. This brief scheduling allows time for you to meet with every child at least once a week

Backpacks

One way to provide extra motivation for reading, and at the same time creatively involve parents and caregivers, is through a take home "Backpack" program. A typical Backpack contains:

* a selection of texts on a common topic

* activities for the child and adults to do together

* a stuffed toy or puppet representing the topic or related character

* a blank journal to use as a log

The child and caregiver use the log to record the activities they've completed and to make suggestions for the next recipient of that Backpack. The log can also include a description of the stuffed animal's adventures during its visit—with accompanying photographs!

Three Little Pigs Backpack

Dear Students,

Hi! I'm one of the Three Pigs. I brought some stories about me and the other two pigs for you to read. I have also found a book about the Wolf and his side of the story. But don't believe a word he says! I'm glad you could spend some time with me this week. The two other Pigs said I can stay with you for the weekend as long as you take good care of me.

In this backpack are several books for us to read and story characters for you to use in retelling the *true* story. Remember to write what we did in the backpack log.

Please be sure to return me on Monday, so I can visit someone else. After you have read all the books, I wonder if you'll believe that Big Bad Wolf or me?

Your Friend,

One of the Three Little Pigs

Dear Parents and Caregivers,

Your child has brought home a backpack with books related to *The Three Little Pigs* and some activities. When you complete the books and activities, please have your child make comments in our backpack log on what he or she did with the Pig this weekend. Don't forget to read other children's comments! On Monday, please check to be sure all the materials are in the backpack and have your child return it to school.

Books:

1. *The Three Little Pigs* by Barry Moser (Little Brown, 2001)
2. *The True Story of the Three Little Pigs* by Jon Scieszka (Scholastic, 1989)
3. *The Three Little Wolves and the Big Bad Pig* by Eugene Trivizas (Scholastic, 1993)
4. *The Three Little Javelinas* by Susan Lowell (Northland, 1992)

Activities:

1. Color and cut out the character stick puppets (enclosed).
2. Retell the story using the stick puppets.
3. Create puppets for a different version of the story.
4. Write your comments in the backpack log.

Special Guest: Pig puppet

I hope you enjoy the books!

Backpacks provide another avenue for exploring favorite authors or class units. We rotate three to five Backpacks each week. The children take the Backpacks home on Thursdays and return them on the following Monday. This allows a few days to restock the backpack's components. Plan your rotations so that each child has at least one Backpack experience every month. The children love using Backpacks to share their reading successes with the special adults in their lives.

The ideas in this chapter focus on text- or meaning-level strategies, which are the heart of strategy instruction. From Author Studies to Backpacks, we've highlighted many ways in which children and adults can share great pieces of literature, as well as a variety of class- and student-created texts. Shared experiences provide the support and scaffolding young children need to become strategic in their reading.

Letter Home

SHARING TEXT

Dear Parents and Caregivers,

Children learn to read with different types of text and varied experiences—one of which is sharing text with others. Sharing text provides support and builds confidence, and it's a great way to model the enjoyment of reading a great book.

Is sharing a text by reading aloud really that important? Reading aloud to young children is one of the most effective ways to cultivate a child's reading development. By reading aloud, adults can model fluent reading and <u>think aloud</u> as they use strategies to comprehend the text. Reading aloud also provides exposure to new vocabulary and opens up new worlds for a child.

When should children read aloud? Whenever they want! Children should be encouraged to share favorite books and poems by reading aloud to peers, family members, and supportive adults. During these interactive sessions, the focus should be on enjoying the experience and not on word-for-word perfection. Young children might choose to "read" by talking about the pictures or putting the story in their own words. As children's reading abilities develop, support them in using a variety of strategies to make meaning from the text.

What is the purpose of whole-group activities? Children need many different grouping formats as part of their literacy instruction. Whole-group, small-group, paired, and individual settings all provide different experiences for each child. Through whole-group activities, your child's teacher can share books that relate to a theme or special author with the entire class and introduce new reading strategies. From these whole-class experiences, the teacher can build other activities that strike a familiar note with the children.

When are children ready for independent reading? Right now! All children can benefit from quiet time spent with a book. While emerging readers might not yet know all of the words in a text, independent reading gives a child the chance to apply strategies he or she is learning in the whole-group setting—and to enjoy a book by a favorite author or on a favorite topic. The key to independent reading is in letting children select their own books, while guiding them to find a book that is not too difficult and not too easy—a book that is just right.

Character **V**enn **D**iagram

_____ and _____

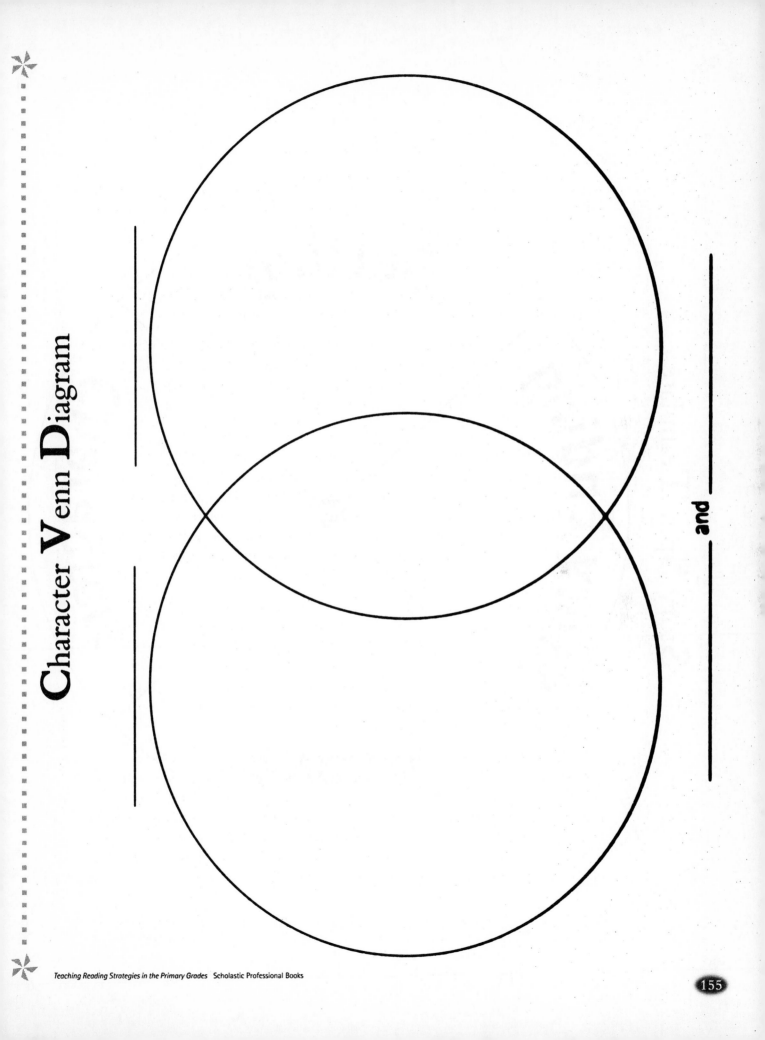

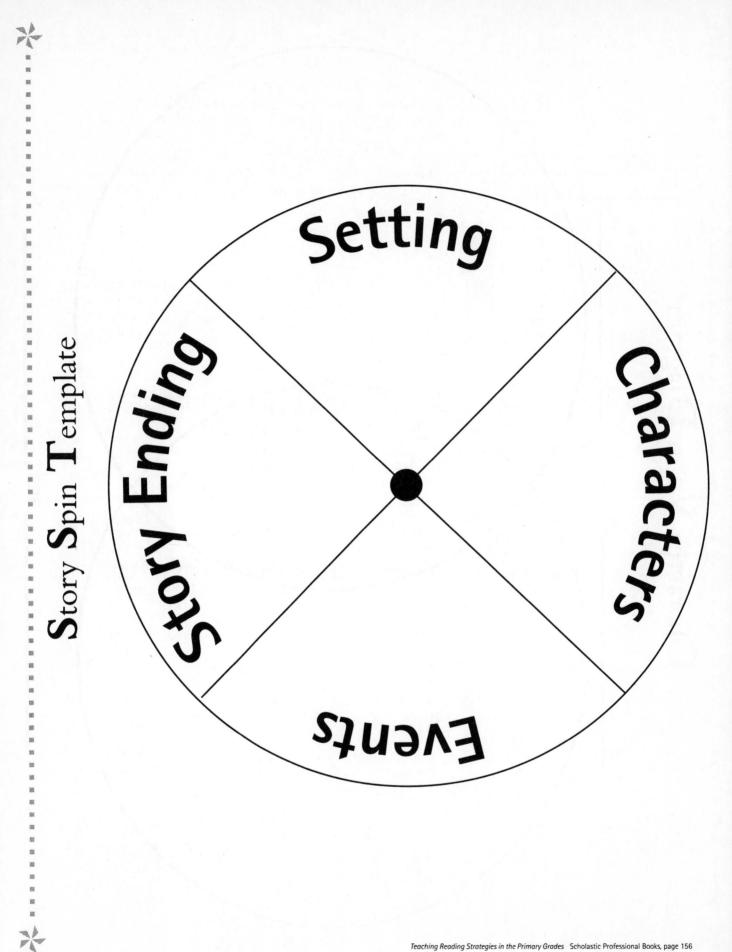

Story Spin Template

Setting

Characters

Events

Story Ending

Pattern for "I Can" Booklet

I can _____ and _____ .

Reading Conference Log

Student's Name: _____ Date: _____

Title: _____ [ ] *Title has been used previously*

Strategies Used	
Checking	
Chunking	
Predicting	
Reading on	
Rereading	
Self-Correcting	
Skipping	
Sliding	
Stretching	
Tracking	

Word Wall Words		
Word Wall Word	Read Successfully	Read Unsuccessfully

Notes Regarding Comprehension

Text Selection	
Text was appropriate	
Text was too difficult	
Text was too easy	

Reading Fluency	
Reading was fluent and expressive	
Reading was choppy (word for word)	
Lack of fluency interrupted meaning	

Plans for future lessons:

Teaching Reading Strategies in the Primary Grades Scholastic Professional Books

Chapter References

Read: *Thinking and Learning about Print*. Champaign, IL: University of Illinois at Urbana-Champaign, 1990.

Coiro, J. "Why Read Aloud?" *Scholastic Early Childhood Today*. 15, no. 2 (October, 2000): 12-14.

Dahl, K. L., Schaver, P. L., Lawson, L. L., and Grogan, P. R. "Phonics Instruction and Student Achievement in Whole Language First-Grade Classrooms" *Reading Research Quarterly*. 34, no. 3 (July/August/September, 1999): 312-341.

Five, C. L., and Dionisio, M. "Organizing for Sensible Skills Instruction." *School Talk*. 4, no. 1 (October, 1998): 1-3, 7.

Gill, S. R. "Reading with Amy: Teaching and Learning through Reading Conferences." *The Reading Teacher*. 53, no. 6 (March, 2000): 500-509.

Lacedonia, N. "Why Do Teachers Read Aloud? Survey of Kindergarten through Grade 12 Teachers." *The New England Reading Association Journal*. 35, no. 1 (Spring, 1999): 16-21.

Manning, M. M. "Conference Call: Enhancing Reading Strategies." *Teaching PreK-8*. 28, no. 8 (May, 1998): 94.

Mastropieri, M. A., Leinart, A., and Scruggs, T. E. "Strategies to Increase Reading Fluency." *Intervention in School and Clinic*. 34, no. 5 (May, 1999): 278-283.

Meyer, M. S., and Felton, R. H. (1999). "Repeated Reading to Enhance Fluency: Old Approaches and New Directions." *Annals of Dyslexia*. 49 (1999): 283-306.

Ouellette, G., Dagostino, L., and Carifio, J. "The Effects of Exposure to Children's Literature through Read Aloud and an Inferencing Strategy on Low Reading Ability Fifth Graders' Sense of Story Structure and Reading Comprehension." *Reading Improvement*. 36, no. 2 (Summer, 1999): 73-89.

Rasinski, T., and Padak, N. *Effective Reading Strategies: Teaching Children Who Find Reading Difficult*. Columbus, OH: Merrill, 2000.

Schulman, M. B., and Payne, C. D. *Guided Reading: Making It Work*. New York: Scholastic, 2000.

Tompkins, G. E. *Literacy for the 21st Century: A Balanced Approach*. Columbus, OH: Merrill, 1997.

Reading Strategy Activities

Accessing— Accessing background knowledge to search for connections between what is known and new information in the text	• A Chapter Books (Chapter 2) • Learning Logs (Chapter 4) • Graphic Organizers (Chapter 4)	• Nonfiction Performances (Chapter 4) • Character Comparisons (Chapter 5)
Analyzing— Analyzing a text for story elements, including characters, events, and setting	• Cereal Mail (Chapter 2) • Chapter Books (Chapter 2) • Learning Logs (Chapter 4) • Graphic Organizers (Chapter 4) • Readers Theater (Chapter 4) • Character Venns (Chapter 5)	• Character Puppets (Chapter 5) • Story Spin (Chapter 5) • Sticky Note Reading (Chapter 5) • Puzzle Pieces (Chapter 5) • Nursery Tales (Chapter 5)
Building fluency— Reading like you talk—focusing on fluency when reading aloud	• Magic Wands (Chapter 1) • Photo Gallery (Chapter 2) • I Can Read (Chapter 2) • Class Book (Chapter 2) • What We Wore (Chapter 2) • Cereal Mail (Chapter 2)	• Chit Chats (Chapter 2) • Fishing (Chapter 3) • Analogies (Chapter 3) • Wordo (Chapter 3) • Board Games (Chapter 3) • Sticker Zoo (Chapter 5)
Checking— Checking picture cues to assist in determining a difficult word	• What We Wore (Chapter 2) • All Around Us (Chapter 2) • Cover-Up (Chapter 5)	• Character Comparisons (Chapter 5) • I Can (Chapter 5)
Chunking— Analyzing words by breaking them into decodable parts; recognizing chunks or patterns of sounds	• All Around Us (Chapter 2) • Special Person Chart Story (Chapter 2) • Language Patterns (Chapter 2) • Rhyming Words (Chapter 3) • Contextual Rhymes (Chapter 3)	• Word Patterns (Chapter 3) • Making Words (Chapter 3) • Analogies (Chapter 3) • Chicken Soup (Chapter 5)
Confirming— Using cues to determine if a word sounds right; accepting the appropriateness of the response	• Special Person Chart Story (Chapter 2) • Word Hunt (Chapter 3) • Mystery Word (Chapter 3)	• Sticky Note Reading (Chapter 5) • Sequencing (Chapter 5)
Cross-Checking— Using resources in the learning environment, such as environmental print, as a reference to confirm a guess	• Morning Message (Chapter 1) • Magic Wands (Chapter 1) • I Can Read (Chapter 2) • All Around Us (Chapter 2) • Chit Chats (Chapter 2) • Lightning Words (Chapter 3) • Word Hunt (Chapter 3) • Mystery Word (Chapter 3)	• Word Jar (Chapter 3) • Wordo (Chapter 3) • Scrabble (Chapter 3) • Learning Logs (Chapter 4) • Chicken Soup (Chapter 5) • Flowcharts (Chapter 5) • Sticky Note Reading (Chapter 5) • Puzzle Pieces (Chapter 5)
Focusing— Distinguishing between important and unimportant information in a text	• Special Person Chart Story (Chapter 2) • Word Riddle (Chapter 3) • Learning Logs (Chapter 4) • Graphic Organizers (Chapter 4)	• Readers Theater (Chapter 4) • Nonfiction Performances (Chapter 4) • Character Venns (Chapter 5)
Forming sounds— Getting your mouth ready to read; focusing on how the mouth is shaped to produce sounds for certain letter cues or patterns	• Magic Wands (Chapter 1) • Photo Gallery (Chapter 2) • Sticker Zoo (Chapter 5)	
Monitoring— Monitoring for understanding by checking to see if the text makes sense	• Special Person Chart Story (Chapter 2) • Rhyming Words (Chapter 3)	• Graphic Organizers (Chapter 4)
Predicting— Using the title and cover illustration to predict what will happen in the text; anticipating content based on prior knowledge	• Name Game (Chapter 2) • Family Interests (Chapter 2)	• Chapter Books (Chapter 2) • Character Comparisons (Chapter 5)

Strategy	Activities	
Previewing— Overviewing the text structure, text cues, pictures, and personal experiences prior to reading a text	• Class Book (Chapter 2) • All Around Us (Chapter 2)	• Notebooks (Chapter 5) • Story Spin (Chapter 5)
Questioning— Asking questions of yourself as you read to monitor for understanding	• Question Markers (Chapter 4) • Graphic Organizers (Chapter 4)	• Nonfiction Performances (Chapter 4) • Cover-Up (Chapter 5)
Rereading— Reading a portion of a text again to build fluency; rereading to use context to correct a miscue or make meaning from text	• Special Person Chart Story (Chapter 2) • Chit Chats (Chapter 2)	• Lightning Words (Chapter 3) • Nursery Tales (Chapter 5)
Self-correcting— Repairing faulty comprehension by correcting a miscue or part of a text	• Special Person Chart Story (Chapter 2)	• Nursery Tales (Chapter 5)
Skipping— Omitting a difficult word—not needed to maintain meaning—and continuing to read	• Cover-Up (Chapter 5)	
Sliding— Beginning with the onset of a word and sliding to the end to help with decoding	• Name Bulletin Board (Chapter 2) • Alphabet Book (Chapter 2) • Name Game (Chapter 2) • All Around Us (Chapter 2) • Chit Chats (Chapter 2)	• Language Patterns (Chapter 2) • Contextual Rhymes (Chapter 3) • Making Words (Chapter 3) • Chicken Soup (Chapter 5)
Stretching— Stretching out each sound of a word in sequence in order to read it	• Name Bulletin Board (Chapter 2) • Alphabet Book (Chapter 2) • Name Sorts (Chapter 2) • Name Game (Chapter 2)	• Special Person Chart Story (Chapter 2) • Chit Chats (Chapter 2) • Language Patterns (Chapter 2) • Making Words (Chapter 3)
Summarizing— Identifying the text sequence or important parts of a text after you read	• Chapter Books (Chapter 2) • Learning Logs (Chapter 4) • Graphic Organizers (Chapter 4) • Readers Theater (Chapter 4) • Puppets (Chapter 4)	• Character Venns (Chapter 5) • Character Puppets (Chapter 5) • Flowcharts (Chapter 5) • Sequencing (Chapter 5)
Synthesizing— Integrating information within and across a text; bringing together separate elements of a text to make a connected and meaningful whole	• Word Riddle (Chapter 3) • Board Games (Chapter 3)	• Learning Logs (Chapter 4) • Sticky Note Reading (Chapter 5)
Thinking aloud— Orally commenting on your thinking processes as you read to maintain or model comprehension	• Name Sorts (Chapter 2) • Interviews (Chapter 2) • Lightning Words (Chapter 3)	• Mystery Word (Chapter 3) • Word Puzzles (Chapter 3) • Cover-Up (Chapter 5)
Tracking (or Pointing)— Using voice-to-print correspondence to match a word you read aloud with a word in print, usually by finger pointing or voice emphasis	• Magic Wands (Chapter 1) • Name Sorts (Chapter 2) • Lightning Words (Chapter 3) • Chicken Soup (Chapter 5)	• Cover-Up (Chapter 5) • I Can (Chapter 5) • Color Booklets (Chapter 5) • Nursery Tales (Chapter 5)
Visualizing— Creating mental visual images to keep your mind focused as you read or listen	• Family Interests (Chapter 2) • Notebooks (Chapter 5) • Color Booklets (Chapter 5) • Sequencing (Chapter 5)	

Book	Related Strategies
Arnold, Tedd. *Five Ugly Monsters*. New York: Scholastic, 1995.	*analyzing, summarizing, synthesizing*
Baker, Keith. *Who is the Beast?* San Diego: Harcourt Brace Jovanovich, 1990.	*checking, predicting*
Bridwell, Norman. *Clifford the Big Red Dog*. New York: Scholastic, 1963.	*analyzing, chunking, cross-checking*
Bridwell, Norman. *Clifford's Riddles*. New York: Scholastic, 1974.	*analyzing, chunking, cross-checking*
Bridwell, Norman. *Clifford Goes to Hollywood*. New York: Scholastic, 1980.	*analyzing, chunking, cross-checking*
Brown, Marc. *Arthur's Valentine*. Boston, MA: Little Brown, 1980.	*accessing, analyzing, checking, predicting, previewing*
Brown, Marc. *Arthur's April Fool*. Boston, MA: Little Brown, 1983.	*accessing, analyzing, checking, predicting, previewing*
Brown, Marc. *Arthur's Halloween*. Boston, MA: Little Brown, 1983.	*accessing, analyzing, checking, predicting, previewing*
Brown, Marc. *Arthur's Thanksgiving*. Boston, MA: Little Brown, 1984.	*accessing, analyzing, checking, predicting, previewing*
Brown, Marc. *Arthur's Christmas*. Boston, MA: Little Brown, 1985.	*accessing, analyzing, checking, predicting, previewing*
Brown, Marc. *Arthur Writes a Story*. Boston, MA: Little Brown, 1998.	*accessing, analyzing, checking, predicting, previewing*
Brown, Marc. *Locked in the Library*. Boston, MA: Little Brown, 1998.	*accessing, analyzing, checking, predicting, previewing*
Brown, M. *Arthur and the Poetry* Contest. Boston, MA: Little Brown, 1999	*accessing, analyzing, checking, predicting, previewing*
Brown, Marc. *Buster's New Friend*. Boston, MA: Little Brown, 2000.	*accessing, analyzing, checking, predicting, previewing*
Brown, M. *Francine the Superstar*. Boston, MA: Little Brown, 2000.	*accessing, analyzing, checking, predicting, previewing*
Canard, Elizabeth. *Munching Mark*, illustrated by Marjory Gardiner. Crystal Lake, IL: Rigby, 1995.	*accessing, analyzing, predicting, summarizing, synthesizing, visualizing*
Cazet, Denys. *Never Spit on Your Shoes*. New York: Orchard, 1990.	*accessing, predicting, previewing*
Christelow, Eileen. *Five Little Monkeys Jumping on the Bed*. Boston, MA: Houghton Mifflin, 1998.	*analyzing, summarizing, synthesizing*
Cutting, Jillian. *Shopping*, photos by Fraser Newman. Bothell, WA: Wright Group, 1996.	*accessing, analyzing, summarizing, synthesizing*
DeGross, Monalisa. *Donavan's Word Jar*, illustrated by Cheryl Hanna. New York: HarperCollins, 1994.	*cross-checking, previewing*
De Regniers, Beatrice Schenk. *How Joe the Bear and Sam the Mouse Got Together*. New York: Lothrop, Lee, & Shepard, 1990.	*analyzing, checking, predicting, summarizing*
Freeman, Don. *Corduroy*. New York: Viking, 1976.	*analyzing, cross-checking, predicting, summarizing*
Ga'g, Wanda. *Millions of Cats*. New York: Scholastic, 1956.	*predicting, rereading, summarizing*
Galdone, Paul. *Henny Penny*. Boston, MA: Houghton Mifflin, 1984.	*analyzing, summarizing*
Geisel, Theodore Seuss. *Green Eggs and Ham*. New York: Random House, 1960.	*chunking, sliding, stretching*
Geisel, Theodore Seuss. *One Fish, Two Fish, Red Fish, Blue Fish*. New York: Random House, 1960.	*chunking, sliding, stretching*
Geisel, Theodore Seuss. *The Lorax*. New York: Random House, 1971.	*predicting, questioning, thinking aloud*
Geisel, Theodore Seuss. *The Butter Battle Book*. New York: Random House, 1984.	*accessing, analyzing, predicting, questioning*
Ginsburg, Mirra. *The Chick and the Duckling*, illustrated by Jose Aruego and Ariane Dewey. New York: Macmillan, 1972.	*cross-checking, predicting, summarizing*
Heke, Carolyn. *Jack de Pert at the Supermarket*, illustrated by Trevor Pye. Bothell, WA: Wright Group, 1993.	*accessing, analyzing, summarizing, synthesizing*
Henkes, Keven. *Chrysanthemum*. New York: Mulberry, 1991.	*accessing, cross-checking*
Keats, Ezra Jack. *Pet Show*. New York: Aladdin, 1987.	*analyzing, checking, predicting*
Keats, Ezra Jack. *Whistle for Willie*. New York: Viking, 1987.	analyzing, checking, predicting
Keats, Ezra Jack. *Goggles!* New York: Puffin, 1998.	*analyzing, checking, predicting*
Lester, Helen. *Tacky the Penguin*, illustrated by Lynn Munsinger. Boston, MA: Houghton Mifflin, 1988.	*analyzing, checking, predicting, summarizing*
Lockyer, John. *Carrots, Peas, and Beans*, illustrated by Lynn Breeze. Bothell, WA: Wright Group, 1996.	*accessing, analyzing, previewing, summarizing, synthesizing*
Lowell, Susan. *The Three Little Javelinas*, illustrated by Jim Harris. Flagstaff, AZ: Northland, 1992.	*analyzing, predicting, synthesizing*
Maass, Robert. *Fire Fighters*. New York: Scholastic, 1989.	*accessing, focusing, previewing, questioning*
Martin, Bill, Jr. *Brown Bear, Brown Bear, What Do You See?*, illustrated by Eric Carle. New York: Henry Holt, 1992.	*building fluency, forming, checking*

Book	Related Strategies
Martin, Bill, Jr., and Archambault, John. *Chicka Chicka Boom Boom*, illustrated by Lois Ehlert. New York: Simon & Schuster, 1991.	*building fluency, forming*
McKee, David. *Elmer*. New York: Lothrop, Lee, and Shepard, 1986.	*predicting, checking*
McVeity, Jen. (1998). *Pop, Pop, Popcorn!*, illustrated by Trish Hill Bothell, WA: Wright Group, 1998.	*accessing, analyzing, sliding, summarizing, synthesizing*
Moser, Barry. *The Three Little Pigs*. Boston, MA: Little Brown, 2001.	*analyzing, predicting, synthesizing*
O'Neill, Mary LeDuc. *Hailstones and Halibut Bones: Adventures in Color*, illustrated by Leonard Weisgard. New York: Doubleday, 1989.	*building fluency, rereading, tracking, visualizing*
Parker, John. *Dad Cooks Breakfast*, illustrated by Brent Putze. Crystal Lake, IL: Rigby, 1998.	*analyzing, checking, summarizing*
Parks, Barbara. *Junie B. Jones and a Little Monkey Business*, illustrated by Denise Brunkus. New York: Random House, 1992.	*accessing, analyzing, predicting, summarizing, synthesizing*
Parks, Barbara. *Junie B. Jones and that Meanie Jim's Birthday*, illustrated by Denise Brunkus. New York: Random House, 1996.	*accessing, analyzing, predicting, summarizing, synthesizing*
Parks, Barbara. *Junie B. Jones is a Graduation Girl*, illustrated by Denise Brunkus. New York: Random House, 2001.	*accessing, analyzing, predicting, summarizing, synthesizing*
Peek, Merle. *Mary Wore her Red Dress and Henry Wore his Green Sneakers*. New York: Clarion, 1985.	*building fluency, checking, cross-checking*
Pritchett, Jan. *Fun Food*, illustrated by Stephen Axelsen. Crystal Lake, IL: Rigby, 1998.	*accessing, analyzing, summarizing, synthesizing*
Pritchett, Jan. *In Norma's Kitchen*, photos by Malcolm Cross. Crystal Lake, IL: Rigby, 1998.	*analyzing, checking, summarizing, synthesizing*
Pritchett, Jan. *What Goes in a Salad?*, illustrated by Marjory Gardner. Crystal Lake, IL: Rigby, 1998.	*accessing, analyzing, checking, summarizing, synthesizing, visualizing*
Pye, Trevor and Wilson, Cherry. *Pizza for Dinner*, illustrated by Trevor Pye. Crystal Lake, IL: Rigby, 1997.	*accessing, analyzing, checking, summarizing, synthesizing, visualizing*
Real Mother Goose, The, illustrated by Blanche Fisher Wright. Chicago, IL: Rand McNally, 1944.	*chunking, cross-checking, rereading, tracking, visualizing*
Rylant, Cynthia. *Henry and Mudge and the Forever Sea*, illustrated by Sucie Stevenson. New York: Aladdin, 1989.	*analyzing, chunking, cross-checking*
Rylant, Cynthia. *Henry and Mudge in the Family Trees*, illustrated by Sucie Stevenson. New York: Aladdin, 1997.	*analyzing, chunking, cross-checking*
Rylant, Cynthia. *Henry and Mudge and the Sneaky Crackers*, illustrated by Sucie Stevenson. New York: Aladdin, 1998.	*analyzing, chunking, cross-checking*
Scieszka, Jon. *The True Story of the Three Little Pigs*, illustrated by Lane Smith. New York: Scholastic, 1989.	*analyzing, predicting, synthesizing*
Sendak, Maurice. *Chicken Soup with Rice*. New York: HarperCollins, 1962.	*chunking, cross-checking, rereading, sliding, tracking*
Silverstein, Shel. *Falling up*. New York: HarperCollins, 1996.	*accessing, chunking, rereading, visualizing*
Stock, Catherine. *Thanksgiving Treat*. New York: Aladdin, 1990.	*checking, confirming, focusing, questioning, thinking aloud*
Trivizas, Eugene. *The Three Little Wolves and the Big Bad Pig*, illustrated by Helen Oxenbury. New York: Scholastic, 1993.	*analyzing, predicting, synthesizing*
Vreeken, Elizabeth. *The Boy Who Would Not Say his Name*. Cleveland, OH: . Modern Curriculum, 1959	*accessing, cross-checking*
Williams, Sue. *I Went Walking*, illustrated by Julie Vivas. San Diego, CA: Harcourt, Brace, Jovanovich, 1989.	*confirming, cross-checking, predicting, summarizing, synthesizing*
Wood, Audrey. (1984). *The Napping House*, illustrated by Don Wood. San Diego, CA: Harcourt, Brace, Jovanovich, 1984.	*analyzing, predicting, summarizing*
Wood, Audrey. *Silly Sally*. San Diego, CA: Harcourt, Brace, Jovanovich, 1992.	*accessing, checking, chunking, rereading, sliding*

Adams, M. J. *Beginning to Read: Thinking and Learning about Print.* Cambridge, MA: MIT, 1990.

Anderson, R. C., Hiebert, E. H., Scott, J. A., and Wilkinson, I. A. G. *Becoming a Nation of Readers: A Report of the Commission on Reading.* Washington, DC: NIE, 1985.

Avery, C. *And with a Light Touch: Learning about Reading, Writing, and Teaching with First Graders.* Portsmouth, NH: Heinemann, 1993.

Bear, D. R., Invernizzi, M., Templeton, S., and Johnston, F. *Words Their Way: Word Study for Phonics, Vocabulary, and Spelling Instruction* (2nd Ed.). Columbus, OH: Merrill, 2000.

Beaver, J. *Developmental Reading Assessment.* Parsippany, NJ: Celebration, 1997.

Clay, M. M. *Reading Recovery: A Guidebook for Teachers in Training.* Portsmouth, NH: Heinemann, 1993.

Cunningham, P. M. *Phonics They Use: Words for Reading and Writing.* New York: HarperCollins, 1995.

Cunningham, P. M. *Systematic Sequential Phonics They Use.* Greensboro, NC: Carson-Dellosa, 2000.

Cunningham, P. M., and Allington, R. L. *Classrooms that Work: They Can All Read and Write.* New York: Longman, 1999.

Cunningham, P. M., and Hall, D. P. *Making Words: Multilevel, Hands-on, Developmentally Appropriate Spelling and Phonics Activities.* Parsippany, NJ: Good Apple, 1994.

Cunningham, P. M., Hall, D. P., and Sigmon, S. M. *The Teacher's Guide to the Four Blocks: A Multimethod, Multilevel Framework for Grades 1-3.* Greensboro, NC: Carson-Dellosa, 1999.

Dahl, K. L., Scharer, P. L., Lawson, L. L., and Grogan, P. R. *Rethinking Phonics: Making the Best Teaching Decisions.* Portsmouth, NH: Heinemann, 2001.

Easter and St. Patrick's Day Thematic Unit. Huntington Beach, CA: Teacher Created Materials, 1992.

Fields, M.V., and Spangler, K.L. *Let's Begin Reading Right: Developmentally Appropriate Beginning Literacy.* Englewood Cliffs, NJ: Prentice-Hall, 1995.

Fitzpatrick, J. *Strategies that Work: Helping Young Readers Develop Independent Reading Skills.* Cypress, CA: Creative Teaching, 1998.

Fleming, M. *25 Holiday and Seasonal Emergent Reader Mini-Books.* Jefferson City, MO: Scholastic, 1998.

Fountas, I. C., and Pinnell, G. S. *Guided Reading: Good First Teaching for all Children.* Portsmouth, NH: Heinemann, 1996.

Fountas, I. C., and Pinnell, G. S. (Eds.). *Voices on Word Matters: Learning about Phonics and Spelling in the Literacy Classroom*. Portsmouth, NH: Heinemann, 1999.

Franco, B. *Write-and-Read Math Story Books*. Jefferson City, MO: Scholastic, 1998.

Gentry, J. R. and Gillet, J. W. *Teaching Kids to Spell*. Portsmouth, NH: Heinemann, 1994.

Hall, K. P. (Ed.). *Learn to Read: Fun and Fantasy Take-Home Books*. Cypress, CA: Creative Teaching, 1997.

Hall, K. P. (Ed.). *Learn to Read: Science Take-Home Books*. Cypress, CA: Creative Teaching, 1997.

Harvey, S., and Goudvis, A. *Strategies that Work: Teaching Comprehension to Enhance Understanding*. York, ME: Stenhouse, 2000.

Jacobson, J., and Raymer, D. *The Big Book of Reproducible Graphic Organizers*. New York: Scholastic, 1999.

Make Your Own Emergent Readers: Going Places. Torrance, CA: Frank Schaffer, 1999.

Make Your Own Emergent Readers: My Friends, My Family and Me. Torrance, CA: Frank Schaffer, 1999.

Make Your Own Emergent Readers: On the Farm. Torrance, CA: Frank Schaffer, 1999.

Moore, H. H. *25 Mother Goose Peek-a-Books*. Jefferson City, MO: Scholastic, 1993.

National Reading Panel. *Report of the National Reading Panel: Teaching Children to Read*. Washington, DC: National Institutes of Health, 2000.

Opitz, M. E. *Learning Centers: Getting Them Started, Keeping Them Going*. New York: Scholastic, 1994.

Pinnell, G. S., and Fountas, I. C. *Word Matters: Teaching Phonics and Spelling in the Reading/Writing Classroom*. Portsmouth, NH: Heinemann, 1998.

Rasinski, T., and Padak, N. *Effective Reading Strategies: Teaching Children Who Find Reading Difficult*. Columbus, OH: Merrill, 2000.

Robillard, V. *Month-by-Month Write and Read Books*. New York: Scholastic, 1999.

Robillard, V. *15 Reproducible Write-and-Read Books*. New York: Scholastic, 1997.

Schulman, M. B., and Payne, C. D. *Guided Reading: Making it Work*. New York: Scholastic Professional Books, 2000.

Sweeney, A. *All About Me Write and Read Books*. Jefferson City, MO: Scholastic, 2000.

Vail, N. J., and Papenfuss, J. F. *Daily Oral Language*. Evanston, IL: McDougal, Littell, 1989.

Allen, L. "An Integrated Strategies Approach: Making Word Identification Instruction Work for Beginning Readers." *The Reading Teacher*. 52, no. 3 (November, 1998): 254-268.

Bond, T. F. "Give Them Free Reign: Connections in Student-Led Book Groups." *The Reading Teacher*. 54, no. 6 (March, 2001): 574-584.

Brabham, E. G., and Villaume, S. K. "Building Walls of Words." *The Reading Teacher*. 54, no. 7 (April, 2001): 700-702.

Bradbury-Wolff, M., and Bergeron, B. S. "Fostering Strategic Readers in a First Grade Classroom." *The Indiana Reading Journal*. 30, no. 3 (Summer, 1998): 6-14.

Dermody, M. M., and Speaker, R. B., Jr. "Reciprocal Strategy Training in Prediction, Clarification, Question Generating and Summarization to Improve Reading Comprehension." *Reading Improvement*. 36, no. 1 (Spring, 1999): 16-23.

Dickinson, D. K., and DiGisi, L. L. "The Many Rewards of a Literacy-Rich Classroom." *Educational Leadership*. 55, no. 6 (March, 1998): 23-6.

Dowhower, S. L. "Supporting a Strategic Stance in the Classroom: A Comprehension Framework for Helping Teachers Help Students to be Strategic." *The Reading Teacher*. 52, no. 7 (April, 1999).

Ediger, M. "Evaluation of Reading Progress." *Reading Improvement*. 36 no. 2 (Summer, 1999): 50-56.

Enz, B., and Serafini, F. "Involving Students in the Assessment Process." *Teaching PreK-8*. 25, no. 5 (March, 1995): 96-97.

Evers, B. J. "Teaching Children to Read and Write." *Principal*. 78, no. 4 (March, 1999): 32-33.

Fielding, L. G., and Pearson, P. D. "Reading Comprehension: What Works." *Educational Leadership*. 51, no. 5 (February, 1994): 62-68.

Frank, C. R., Dixson, C. N., and Brandts, L. R. "Bears, Trolls, and Pagemakers: Learning about Learners in Book Clubs." *The Reading Teacher*. 54, no. 5 (February, 2001): 448-462.

Fry, E. (1998). "The Most Common Phonograms." *The Reading Teacher*. 51, no. 7 (April, 1998): 622.

Gambrell, L. B. "What Motivates Children to Read?" *Scholastic Literacy Research Paper*. 2 (1994).

Headley, K. N., and Dunston, P. J. "Teacher's Choices Books and Comprehension Strategies as Transaction Tools." *The Reading Teacher*. 54, no. 3 (November, 2000): 260-268.

Leland, C., and Fitzpatrick, R. "Cross-age Interaction Builds Enthusiasm for Reading and Writing." *The Reading Teacher.* 47, no. 4 (December/January, 1993/1994): 292-301.

Moser, G.P. and Morrison, T. G. "Increasing Students' Achievement and Interest in Reading." *Reading Horizons.* 38, no. 4 (March/April, 1998): 233-245.

Price, D. P. "Explicit Instruction at the Point of Use." *Language Arts.* 76, no. 1 (September, 1998): 19-26.

Rose, M. C. "Don't Stop Now: A Call to Parents to Read Aloud to Your Children—No Matter What Their Age." *Instructor.* 108, no. 8 (May/June, 1999): 28.

Scarcelli, S. M., and Morgan, R. F. "The Efficacy of Using a Direct Reading Instruction Approach in Literature Based Classrooms." *Reading Improvement.* 36, no. 4 (Winter, 1999): 172-179.

Schwaartz, R. M. "Self-Monitoring in Beginning Reading." *The Reading Teacher.* 51, no. 1 (September, 1997): 40-48.

Tompkins, G. E. "Literature-Based Reading Instruction: What's Guiding the Instruction?" *Language Arts.* 72, no. 6 (October, 1995): 405-414.

Wagstaff, J. M. "Building Practical Knowledge of Letter-Sound Correspondences: A Beginner's Word Wall and Beyond." *The Reading Teacher.* 51, no. 4 (December/January, 1997/1998): 298-304.

Wang, C-C., and Gaffney, J. S. "First Graders' Use of Analogy in Word Reading." *Journal of Literacy Research.* 30, no. 3 (September, 1998): 389-403.

Instructional Material Checklist

_____ Adhesive notes

_____ Backpacks

_____ Binders or notebooks

_____ Book crates or baskets (one per table)

_____ Briefcase (filled with writing supplies)

_____ Butcher paper

_____ Chart paper (lined and unlined)

_____ Cover-up tape

_____ Easel (free-standing)

_____ Environmental print samples

_____ File folders (assorted colors)

_____ Grid paper

_____ Hardware organizer (for word tiles)

_____ Highlighting tape

_____ Index cards (various sizes)

_____ Lined paper (student)

_____ Magic wands (e.g., fly swatters, cat teasers)

_____ Overhead transparencies (blanks)

_____ Pocket chart

_____ Popsicle sticks

_____ Puppets

_____ Puzzle pieces

_____ Sentence strips

_____ Shoeboxes (plastic or cardboard)

_____ Stickers or clipart

_____ Story paper

_____ Story props

_____ Stuffed animals (story characters)

_____ Tagboard